GOD
CALLS
YOU
forgiven

180
DEVOTIONS
AND PRAYERS
TO INSPIRE
YOUR SOUL

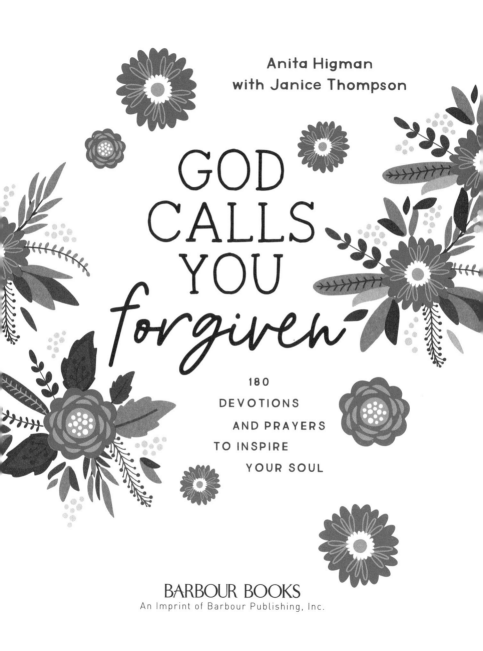

Anita Higman
with Janice Thompson

GOD CALLS YOU
forgiven

180
DEVOTIONS
AND PRAYERS
TO INSPIRE
YOUR SOUL

BARBOUR BOOKS
An Imprint of Barbour Publishing, Inc.

Member of the
Evangelical Christian
Publishers Association

Printed in China.

introduction

One of the gravest dangers to our souls and to the world is believing that we are fairly decent people at heart. That we are somehow good enough on our own and that we don't really need forgiveness. Well, if someone put our thoughts and hidden actions up on a big screen for the whole world to see, that notion of our own natural goodness would inevitably crumble like the walls of Jericho!

But who then has the authority to forgive sins? Who has proven Himself worthy with the most profound sacrifice and the purest love? Jesus Christ. What was covered in the darkness of depravity has now seen the dawn of redemption. Because of Jesus, a world that was bent on destruction and pride and despair is now flushed with hope and joy!

May we all keep company with this God-man named Jesus, and in that intimate walk, may we come to know the freedom and the courage to grow into the beautiful creatures God meant us to be.

–Anita Higman

GLIMPSES OF GLORY

*If we confess our sins, he is faithful and just and will
forgive us our sins and purify us from all unrighteousness.*
1 JOHN 1:9 NIV

Penelope adored Italy, and when she'd finally saved enough pennies, she flew there on vacation. The moment she stepped out of the airport she knew she was about to experience the most glorious journey of her life. There was only one problem. Penelope didn't know what to do with all her luggage. She didn't like leaving her belongings in her hotel room, so she carried her heavy backpack and pulled her even heavier baggage up and down the streets. The shop owners looked aghast when she tried to slog her way through their shelves of dainty souvenirs. Oh, and forget about hiking in the mountains dragging all those clumsy bags behind her. As it turned out, most of her dream holiday was spent guarding her junk. Stressed and tired from lack of trust, she saw little, visited less, and enjoyed nothing.

Too many days we live like Penelope, dragging around old forgiven sins because we can't seem to trust the Lord and believe they're pardoned. When we're busy guarding our old junk, we miss our finest hours and our greatest adventures. We experience only glimpses of glory when we were meant for so much more.

*Lord, help me to know with certainty that
You have forgiven all of my sins. Amen.—AH*

YOUR MERCY ENDURES

*"Therefore I tell you, her sins, which are many, are
forgiven—for she loved much. But he who is forgiven little,
loves little." And he said to her, "Your sins are forgiven."*
LUKE 7:47–48 ESV

In high school, Stacy ran with a rough crowd, and then as an adult she fell into a destructive pattern of behaviors, which included addictions, thievery, and sexual promiscuity. When Stacy hit bottom after an abortion, she thought of taking her own life.

In the midst of her misery, a woman in a coffee shop befriended her and told her of a fresh start in Christ. But why would Jesus forgive her? Hadn't she gone way too far to ever turn back now? When the woman explained that all of humanity has fallen far from where we were meant to be, Stacy paused to think on it. When she fully understood the love and mercy and power of Christ, Stacy's eyes blurred with tears. She had never known love or freedom—certainly not the beautiful and real kind. And she had never possessed the power to walk away from sin—but she did now.

Stacy loved hearing the words of Christ, ancient and yet so near to her spirit, "Your sins are forgiven." Her soul nearly burst with love for this God-man named Jesus, who gave her the first and best hope her soul had ever known.

*Thank You, Lord, for forgiving my many sins.
I love You deeply. Amen.—AH*

THE WRONG PATH

I appeal to you, brothers, to watch out for those who cause divisions and create obstacles contrary to the doctrine that you have been taught; avoid them. For such persons do not serve our Lord Christ, but their own appetites, and by smooth talk and flattery they deceive the hearts of the naive.

ROMANS 16:17–18 ESV

Smooth talkers. Hmmm. We've all met 'em. Maybe people who stir up trouble and entice us with teachings that are contrary to what we know is in God's Holy Word should each come with a little red warning sticker over their mouth!

As a society we have now seen every kind of divisive hate-speech and spiritual folly, including those who would like us to think that we don't even need forgiveness for our sins. Romans 3:23 (ESV) reminds us, "For all have sinned and fall short of the glory of God." And Isaiah 5:20 (ESV) tells us, "Woe to those who call evil good and good evil, who put darkness for light and light for darkness, who put bitter for sweet and sweet for bitter!" Yes, we do indeed need forgiveness for our sins, and we also must guard our hearts so that we are not led down the wrong paths and someday need a warning label over our own mouths!

Lord, may I never be led astray by false prophets or unbiblical doctrines! Amen.–AH

GOOD AND HUMBLE

*Therefore, as God's chosen people, holy and
dearly loved, clothe yourselves with compassion,
kindness, humility, gentleness and patience.*
COLOSSIANS 3:12 NIV

When a woman is forgiven and free in Christ, how does that translate into everyday human reality? It might be a bit humorous to see what it *doesn't* look like. Say there's a neighborhood play group your little girl loves to be a part of, but whenever you see that one "supermom" headed your way, you always shrink like 100 percent cotton in a red-hot dryer. Yeah, that supermom wafts around wearing the perfume of having her act together—every minute of every day—even in her sleep. She can cook, clean, play, teach, shop, garden, doctor, chauffeur, and volunteer circles around you. And she lets you know it with every look, comment, and hoist of her nose. So you cower in her presence in your clammy mess of a sweatshirt—which you haven't washed in weeks—and you pray hard that you can come to know a tidier life while Supermom comes to know a humbler spirit. Both seem impossible, but you are going to put your trust where it belongs.

*Dear God, please help me to be a really good mom.
And show me how to clothe myself in compassion,
kindness, humility, gentleness, and patience.
In Jesus' name I pray. Amen.—AH*

FRAIL, FICKLE, AND FALLIBLE

Every good gift and every perfect gift is from above,
coming down from the Father of lights, with whom
there is no variation or shadow due to change.
JAMES 1:17 ESV

Emily rested against her favorite tree and watched as each breeze changed the shadowy patterns of the leaves on the ground. With every puff of air, the design changed, never the same. When it comes to our natural surroundings, those dancing, swaying shapes can be fun to watch. Even relaxing in a way. But if you infuse a relationship with that same kind of shifty nature, it may come off like unpredictability and instability. Not so delightful. We want relationships to be as solid as the trunk of a healthy tree, not like the flighty, flickering leaves or their shadows. Because our earthly relationships are comprised of spiritually frail, fickle, and fallible people, many times they are not what they should be. Oh, how we can rejoice that God's character is holy. He does not shift like shadows. He will not fail us. When God makes a promise, He keeps it. When God loves, He does it like the whole of the universe is counting on it. Because it is.

So if God says we are forgiven when we ask, then we are forgiven indeed. May we always live like it!

Lord, thank You for forgiving me for all my sins.
I believe You and will take You at Your word. Amen.–AH

DON'T FORGET YOUR ANVIL!

"Take my yoke upon you and learn from me, for I am gentle and humble in heart, and you will find rest for your souls. For my yoke is easy and my burden is light."
MATTHEW 11:29-30 NIV

Moms are great. They make sure you have what you need for school—that is, your lunch, your homework, and some hugs to carry you through the day. But what if your mom yahooed to you, "Honey, don't forget your anvil! That should fit in your backpack just fine. Oh, and let me help you strap on those mini sandbags around the bottoms of your jeans. You can never have too much weight for the day!" What?

But isn't that a bit like what we do spiritually when we weigh ourselves and our families down with worries and woes that we were never meant to carry? We can't pull it off. We try hard. But alas, we fail. Every single time. When will we get it? Give it up. Empty that load at the cross. The worries. The doubts. The future. All of it. Our Lord can handle it.

Lord, I officially give You all my weights and burdens.
I can't carry them anymore. Show me how to
walk with You and live lightly. Amen.—AH

BRINGING HIM DELIGHT

*But when they heard it, they went away one by one,
beginning with the older ones, and Jesus was left alone with
the woman standing before him. Jesus stood up and said to
her, "Woman, where are they? Has no one condemned you?"
She said, "No one, Lord." And Jesus said, "Neither do I
condemn you; go, and from now on sin no more."*
JOHN 8:9–11 ESV

Maryellen, the wife of a prominent politician, loved to go to parties. She loved the attention, the glamour, the gowns, everything. But sometimes her husband noticed that she got carried away when some of the men flirted with her. After one of the parties, he confronted her. Maryellen wept in sorrow over her careless behavior and humbly apologized for the hurt she'd caused him. She promised in the future to be on her guard so as not to compromise her integrity or his. When Maryellen headed to the next party, within minutes she was already giggling and flirting up a storm. What happened? Did Maryellen care more about her own fleeting pleasures than the love and respect she had for her husband?

If we keep going back to our sins again and again, how is that a good way to thank and love Jesus for His forgiveness and His unfailing love?

*Dear Lord, I confess my sins before You. Please give me
the courage and will and power to walk away from all
the things that do not bring You delight. Amen.—AH*

THE STONES WILL CRY OUT

When he came near the place where the road goes down the Mount of Olives, the whole crowd of disciples began joyfully to praise God in loud voices for all the miracles they had seen: "Blessed is the king who comes in the name of the Lord!" "Peace in heaven and glory in the highest!" Some of the Pharisees in the crowd said to Jesus, "Teacher, rebuke your disciples!" "I tell you," he replied, "if they keep quiet, the stones will cry out."

LUKE 19:37–40 NIV

This passage in Luke may make you wonder what it could really mean. But our Lord has authority over all that He has made, and if He had chosen to, Jesus had the power to make all of creation shout praise that day as He was riding into Jerusalem. Jesus is worthy of our praise and thanksgiving for all that He has done. Sometimes we squeak like mice when we should roar like lions. Sometimes we forget who we belong to. We are children of the King of kings and the Lord of lords! And we will live with Him forever and ever. Hallelujah!

We have much to celebrate. We are forgiven and cherished by the Maker of all creation. May the stones never need to cry out because we are busy thanking and praising and loving and singing and living out His beautiful grace.

Lord Jesus, thank You for Your mercy and grace. May I never stop singing Your praises! Amen.—AH

FINDING MERCY

*Whoever tries to hide his sins will not succeed,
but the one who confesses his sins and leaves
them behind will find mercy.*
PROVERBS 28:13 VOICE

The little boy, Simon, did it again. He blew it. This time he got steaming mad at his baby sister for coloring on his homework, so to retaliate he tossed one of her silly pink froglet toys into the toilet. And if that wasn't quite enough damage—well, he flushed. Then he did what he always did after a naughty deed: he hid in his room. Two minutes later came the high-pitched shrieks from his baby sister. Then his mom came into his room and found him. Mom was crying. She looked tired and unhappy. Why had he done it? While he was given some "thinking time" in the corner, he had some big boy thoughts. Like, *Maybe I shouldn't hide when I do something bad. Mom will find me anyway. Or maybe I should just go to Mom and talk to her about all the stuff that my baby sister does to drive me crazy.*

Maybe we should all ponder what Simon pondered. God is going to find us anyway. . . .

Father God, help me not to sin. But when I do something bad, please remind me that it is better to run to You for forgiveness than hide in the darkness. In Jesus' name I pray. Amen.–AH

MAY I REMEMBER

When he saw them, he said, "Go, show yourselves to the priests." And as they went, they were cleansed. One of them, when he saw he was healed, came back, praising God in a loud voice. He threw himself at Jesus' feet and thanked him—and he was a Samaritan. Jesus asked, "Were not all ten cleansed? Where are the other nine? Has no one returned to give praise to God except this foreigner?"

LUKE 17:14–18 NIV

The reason our mothers taught us to say please and thank you is because it is the polite thing to do. As adults we sometimes let these courtesies slip from our daily activities, and yet they are important. After all, to say thank you means we received something of value, whether it be someone's time or money or kindness. Perhaps to say thanks is like a tiny humbling of the soul—that is, to admit we've been helped. Or it means we must acknowledge that we are not all-powerful and self-sufficient. Why would we deny anyone our gratitude? Could our lack of thankfulness stem from a smidgen of thoughtlessness or busyness or even pride?

When Jesus healed ten leapers and only one came back to say thanks, He wondered where the other nine were. Would they not bother to say to their Healer, "Thank You"?

Lord, I know You have given me everything,
including healing and forgiveness and eternal life.
May I remember to say thank You! Amen.—AH

GREATNESS

At that time the disciples came to Jesus and asked,
"Who is the greatest in the kingdom of heaven?" He called
a child, whom he put among them, and said, "Truly I tell
you, unless you change and become like children,
you will never enter the kingdom of heaven."
<small>MATTHEW 18:1–3 NRSV</small>

The professor sat a bit smugly at his desk. Behind him on the wall was a display of his life—degrees, books, accolades, including a doctorate in theology. Sometimes he wondered, though, if the display wasn't so much a testament to his dedication to teaching and nurturing his students as a tribute to his pomposity.

Meanwhile, the professor noticed a little girl and her father playing outside together in the park. The girl suddenly picked a wildflower and placed it on her father's head, which made them both laugh. The scene seemed a little silly to the professor, and yet he remained spellbound. The relationship between the girl and her dad seemed trusting, guileless, and truly loving. Right there in the park, the girl hollered, "I love you, Daddy!"

After watching the scene, the professor realized that he'd indeed lost the original inspiration he had for his profession as well as the passion in his spiritual walk with God. The moment turned into an epiphany that day, and it became as deeply rooted in his soul as it was freeing.

Lord, show me how to become like a child again. Amen.—AH

THE PALMS OF HIS HANDS

*Eternal One: Is it possible for a mother, however
disappointed, however hurt, to forget her nursing child?
Can she feel nothing for the baby she carried and birthed?
Even if she could, I, God, will never forget you.
Look here. I have made you a part of Me,
written you on the palms of My hands.*
ISAIAH 49:15–16 VOICE

When people want to make a gift extra special and memorable, they
sometimes have it engraved. These markings with loving words or initials
or names not only make the gift a one-of-a-kind present, but turn it into
a precious heirloom to be passed down from generation to generation.
Perhaps you have a bracelet, and you want to have a love note carved
inside or two sets of names intertwining to express your forever love.

In this passage in Isaiah, God is not only talking about the Israelites;
He is talking about each of us. God loves us so passionately, He writes
our names on the palms of His hands. God took that divine engraving
one step further. His Son, Jesus, still has the nail prints on His palms to
prove His sacrifice on our behalf, His redemption of us, and His forever
love for us. Imagine. . .

*My Creator God, I accept and thank You for Your
redemption. I am glad You love me and will never
forget me! In Jesus' name I pray. Amen.–AH*

ISN'T THAT MARY'S SON?

*The next Sabbath he began teaching in the synagogue,
and many who heard him were amazed. They asked,
"Where did he get all this wisdom and the power to perform
such miracles?" Then they scoffed, "He's just a carpenter, the
son of Mary and the brother of James, Joseph, Judas, and
Simon. And his sisters live right here among us." They were
deeply offended and refused to believe in him. Then Jesus told
them, "A prophet is honored everywhere except in his own
hometown and among his relatives and his own family."*

MARK 6:2-4 NLT

Ellie witnessed the first day of spring from her porch swing—warm sun, cool breeze, and flowers irresistibly lush and fragrant. But suddenly, Ellie stomped back into the house, slammed the door, and decided not to enjoy a day made in heaven. Ellie's stubbornness was going to make her miss paradise. Why?

That is a bit like the way Jesus was treated in His hometown when He preached. They slammed the door on His Good News. Was it the familiarity? Stubbornness? Pride? So who do we say Jesus is? Was He a mere man who managed a few magic tricks? Or is He truly the Son of God—full of wisdom and majesty and power—who gave His life for us and has the authority to forgive our sins?

Lord, may I always acknowledge who You really are! Amen.—AH

19

SHE THRASHED A LOT

We also pray that you will be strengthened with all his glorious power so you will have all the endurance and patience you need. May you be filled with joy, always thanking the Father. He has enabled you to share in the inheritance that belongs to his people, who live in the light.
COLOSSIANS 1:11–12 NLT

When our days on this side of eternity come to a close, each one of us will remain as memories in the lives of various people, whether family, friends, acquaintances, coworkers, or people who merely crossed our paths once upon a time. How will we be remembered? Will people recall us mostly as Christ followers who thrashed about, impatient with life and the people around us? Will our complaining and whining come to mind first before our love or good deeds? Oh dear. Or will we be remembered as courageous women of faith who might not have been perfect but who lived like we were indeed forgiven and free and loved by our Lord? The latter sounds quite beautiful, doesn't it?

We have a daily choice how we will live for God. . . .

Heavenly Father, I want people to have good memories of me. To remember that I lived a life for You. That I not only witnessed to people about Your Good News but truly lived like I was forgiven and free. In Jesus' name I pray. Amen.–AH

WHO CAN REFUSE SUCH LOVE?

*But now thus says the LORD, he who created you, O Jacob,
he who formed you, O Israel: "Fear not, for I have redeemed
you; I have called you by name, you are mine."*

ISAIAH 43:1 ESV

The cute couple was flushed with love. The sweethearts carved their initials in a tree. They kissed under an arbor of roses. They danced in the rain and whispered sweet nothings in the moonlight. They sent each other ridiculously gooey messages day and night. They were hopelessly and giddily and fervently in love. But when the boyfriend was asked if he was willing–today, right now–to die for his girlfriend, he made a flicker of a pause. Eventually, he backed away. Then the man wept, for he realized his love had limits.

God says, not just to His chosen people Israel, but to all of us, "You are mine." The Lord woos us. The Lord wants to love us, challenge us, forgive us, inspire us, protect us, guide us, and cherish us. And He wants us to love Him in return. When it came to the ultimate love-test, Jesus willingly gave up His life for us. For you.

How can we refuse such love?

*Jesus, thank You for loving me so much that You gave up
Your life for me so that I might be saved! Amen.—AH*

WHO AM I?

When someone becomes a Christian, he becomes
a brand new person inside. He is not the same
anymore. A new life has begun!

2 CORINTHIANS 5:17 TLB

Have you ever slogged through life—just going through the motions—and then, as if waking from a dream, asked, "Who am I anyway?" Some days you feel like you know what you're about and nothing can stop you, and then all at once you realize you are but a breath—and maybe a foul breath at that! The world's mixed signals make us crazy—like we're wonderful today but tomorrow we might become worthless. And even some scriptures confuse us. Some verses tell us that we are like chaff in the wind, that our hearts are deceitful, and that all our deeds are like filthy rags. Then other scriptures remind us that we are daughters of the King of kings, and we will inherit the kingdom of God!

So who are we really? In Romans 3:23-24 (TLB), we read, "Yes, all have sinned; all fall short of God's glorious ideal; yet now God declares us 'not guilty' of offending him if we trust in Jesus Christ, who in his kindness freely takes away our sins." Yes, we are sinners, but when we accept Christ, we become new creatures in Him. A new life has indeed begun!

Lord, thank You for being patient with me as
You mold me into a new creation! Amen.—AH

COMEDY OF ERRORS

I have told you these things, so that in Me you may have [perfect] peace and confidence. In the world you have tribulation and trials and distress and frustration; but be of good cheer [take courage; be confident, certain, undaunted]! For I have overcome the world. [I have deprived it of power to harm you and have conquered it for you.]
JOHN 16:33 AMPC

Misunderstandings. With that one word, visions immediately come dancing into your head, and they sure aren't of sugar plums! They might go like this. You text someone, and they don't "get it." You were just trying to make a joke, but it fell flat. You send a message back, but in your haste, you somehow make it worse. Suddenly, it seems like nobody thinks you're funny, and everybody on planet Earth is mad at you! Sigh. Whether your distress is exaggerated in your mind or is a very real tribulation, life is not easy. Sometimes life doesn't feel like a comedy of errors but more like a tragedy in the making. Even as forgiven creatures in Christ, we will still have trials in this world. But the good news is that Christ has overcome the world, and He promises never to leave us or forsake us.

Life is hard, Lord. I'm so glad You are with me to help me every minute of every day! Amen.–AH

THE MYSTERY OF FORGIVENESS

Under the whole heaven he lets it go, and his lightning to the corners of the earth. After it his voice roars; he thunders with his majestic voice, and he does not restrain the lightnings when his voice is heard. God thunders wondrously with his voice; he does great things that we cannot comprehend.

JOB 37:3–5 ESV

God is majestic and powerful and mysterious. Yet He can be our most intimate friend. He is everywhere, yet He can live in my heart and yours. He can talk to us in any way He chooses, since all of creation is under His divine authority. He can reach out to us through the Bible, visions, miracles, angels, dreams, people, prayer, books, signs and wonders, music, prophets, worship, or even nature as we read in Job.

The point is, God does wondrous things that we cannot fully understand. Even forgiveness contains some mystery. Who has the authority and power to forgive sins? The Messiah. The Son of God. The Anointed One. Jesus Christ, who offered up His life for us that we might know redemption and live forever with God. Yes, forgiveness seems unfathomable, yet it is real and beautiful and ours for the asking.

Almighty God, I am in awe of Your majesty, but I am warmed by Your love for me. Thank You for the miracle of redemption. I accept Your forgiveness! In Jesus' name I pray. Amen.—AH

FORGIVING OTHERS

*Love is very patient and kind, never jealous or envious,
never boastful or proud, never haughty or selfish or rude.
Love does not demand its own way. It is not irritable or
touchy. It does not hold grudges and will hardly
even notice when others do it wrong.*

1 CORINTHIANS 13:4–5 TLB

There is no getting around it—grudges put off a nasty odor. Not so much in the air, but in our spirits. Grudges tend to hang around and muck up not only the surroundings but people's lives. Sometimes for as long as they live. And for what reason? What can be gained by holding a grudge? Does it give us a sense of pride or revenge? Does it bring us closer to God? Does if offer us peace and joy? As believers, what can we truly gain by holding a grudge other than giving ourselves stress and potential illness and grieving the Holy Spirit who lives inside us? Not good. What *is* good is the freedom obtained when we forgive others. Ephesians 4:32 (TLB) says it well: "Be kind to each other, tenderhearted, forgiving one another, just as God has forgiven you because you belong to Christ." Now that kind of attitude will be cleansing to the spirit—as pleasant as a cooling breeze and as refreshing as a spring shower!

*Lord, help me to forgive all those who have wronged me.
I want to live free, and I want to please You. Amen.—AH*

HEAVEN'S POETRY

For we are the product of His hand, heaven's poetry etched
on lives, created in the Anointed, Jesus, to accomplish
the good works God arranged long ago.
EPHESIANS 2:10 VOICE

Each day is a blank canvas. A fresh writing tablet. A silent void waiting to be filled with the lyrics and melody of a new song. We long to make things because God is the Creator of all things, and we are made in His image. We have a yearning deep in our souls not just to create, but to design things of beauty along with God. Yes, even if our hearts refuse to admit it, that yearning is ever there.

Don't we also delight in making things with our kids? What satisfaction there is to be had when we work on a fun project with our children. It's not just the simple act of creating but being in each other's company while working together that brings such joy. Likewise, God delights in us as we share our work with Him. Yes indeed, heaven's poetry has been etched on our very lives. May that poetry glorify God and bring delight to all!

Creator God, I am so happy You have made me in Your
image and given me purpose. When we work together,
play together, create together, I am full of delight, and
I know You are too. In Jesus' name I pray. Amen.–AH

THAT IRRESISTIBLE GOODNESS!

Oh, taste and see that the LORD is good!
Blessed is the man who takes refuge in him!
PSALM 34:8 ESV

Harvesttime has arrived, and your tiny orchard of pears is ripe and ready for picking. The sunlight plays along the greenish golden skin, then curls its way around the fruit, almost winking at you. You laugh, feeling a little silly. And yet. Such anticipation of God's bountiful offerings is hard to shrug off. You reach up and pluck a pear from a weighted branch. And your spirit lightens as you breathe in the heady perfume and the "knowing" of just how juicy and sweet it will be. Mmm.

Yes, taste and eat the fruit that God has provided. It is good for sustenance, for sharing, and for the sheer beauty of holding it, smelling it, and maybe even featuring it in a still life painting. God provides good things in every season. All the days of our lives, may we taste the Lord and know the irresistible goodness of Him!

Almighty God, I run into Your arms when I am downtrodden,
and I indeed find refuge in You. Your mercy and forgiveness
and goodness are all around me, and I find that I am truly
blessed. I love You dearly! In Jesus' name I pray. Amen.—AH

HURRY SICKNESS

"Be still, and know that I am God. I will be exalted among the nations, I will be exalted in the earth!"
PSALM 46:10 ESV

Hurry sickness is a malady of the mind that causes people to dash to and fro, always checking their watches. These poor folks can't seem to relax. They must be ever doing something, never just "being." Wow, sounds like most of America! What could cause such a condition?

Our world is accustomed to seeing time as limited units and not as an infinite stream. Because God is eternal, He sees time very differently than we do. The enemy of our souls wants us so rushed and stressed and ill and tired that we can't do the Lord's will or ever find delight in our days. First Kings 19:12 (AMPC) says it beautifully: "And after the earthquake a fire, but the Lord was not in the fire; and after the fire [a sound of gentle stillness and] a still, small voice."

Hurry sickness can keep us from hearing the still, small voice of God. Think of it this way: if you're forever hurrying, life becomes a blur, and you will miss the happy and holy surprises that sometimes arrive in those packages of unhurried quiet.

Lord, if I'm suffering from hurry sickness, please help me. I want to live free! Amen.—AH

HOW SHALL I LIVE?

How should we respond to all of this? Is it good to persist
in a life of sin so that grace may multiply even more?
Absolutely not! How can we die to a life where sin ruled
over us and then invite sin back into our lives?
ROMANS 6:1-2 VOICE

Linette heard her daughter's bloodcurdling scream and raced to her bedroom. Her daughter sat quietly reading. Linette said, "What's wrong? You scared the liver out of me." The girl looked up with a gleam in her eye and said she wanted to frighten her just for fun. She knew her mom would forgive her no matter what, so she was seeing how far she could go with that idea.

Hmm. Linette quickly set her daughter straight. Yes, she would be forgiven, but to keep doing bad stuff so that she could watch her mom forgive over and over and over, well, that wasn't really a Christlike thing to do. Maybe her daughter had misunderstood the passage in Romans 6 when they had their family devotions. We shouldn't persist in doing bad stuff so that we can watch all the mercies pile up!

Later, though, Linette wondered how many times she had done the same thing to God.

Lord, I love Your forgiveness, but I don't want to abuse Your
generous mercy. Please help me to stop my transgressions
so that I will no longer grieve Your Holy Spirit. Amen.—AH

WHO CAN THROW A STONE?

They said to him, "Teacher, this woman has been caught in the act of adultery. Now in the Law, Moses commanded us to stone such women. So what do you say?" This they said to test him, that they might have some charge to bring against him. Jesus bent down and wrote with his finger on the ground. And as they continued to ask him, he stood up and said to them, "Let him who is without sin among you be the first to throw a stone at her."

JOHN 8:4–7 ESV

For the woman who'd been caught in adultery and faced a group of accusers who wanted her stoned, Jesus forever altered her life—and theirs. The Lord gave the perfect answer. To paraphrase, "If you are without sin, then you may throw the first stone." They all had to walk away. Every last one of them. Why? Because they were all guilty. Just like today. We are sinners in need of a redeemer. We try to find a savior in a thousand and one creative ways, but only One can truly save us—the One who gave His life for us, who paid the price for our sins, and who conquered death with a miraculous resurrection. There is just one Savior of the world—Jesus—and He is the only One who can turn our horror into heaven!

Thank You, Lord, for rescuing me
from my life of sin. Amen.—AH

THE INVITATION

*Then the King will say to those to His right, **King:** Come here,
you beloved, you people whom My Father has blessed.
Claim your inheritance, the Kingdom prepared
for you from the beginning of creation.*
MATTHEW 25:34 VOICE

Once upon a time there was a young man who lived in the shadows of
a palace. He slept in the woods, lived off scraps of food thrown out to
the animals, and sometimes even stole valuables from the palace. Then
one day, the owner of the palace strode over to the young man before
he could run away, and he hugged him as if they were old friends. The
owner said, "I have decided to give you a set of keys to my palace.
What do you think of that? And I'm giving you a formal invitation to
dine with me this evening. I hope you will come. Please!" Then he let
out a friendly chuckle before returning inside.

The young man stepped back in shock, not knowing how to reply.
How could he sit at the table with this man? After all, he had committed
countless offenses against him. Worried that the invitation was a trap
rather than a real pardon, the young man fled. But something drew
him back. Perhaps it was the mercy he witnessed in the owner's eyes.

*Lord Jesus, please help people to see that when they refuse Your
grace, they are giving up the keys to Your kingdom. Amen.—AH*

LIGHT-BEARERS

"Here's another way to put it: You're here to be light,
bringing out the God-colors in the world. God is not a
secret to be kept. We're going public with this, as public as
a city on a hill. If I make you light-bearers, you don't think
I'm going to hide you under a bucket, do you? I'm putting
you on a light stand. Now that I've put you there on a hilltop,
on a light stand—shine! Keep open house; be generous with
your lives. By opening up to others, you'll prompt people
to open up with God, this generous Father in heaven."
MATTHEW 5:14-16 MSG

The world is miserably lost in the dark. People stumble around and bang into things and hurt themselves. Sometimes they scream out in pain. Odd thing is, many stubbornly continue to live a life of anguish even when they know they can't find their own way. As followers of Christ, we are light-bearers of His grace. We are to carry that illumination with us daily. Even when we're not witnessing about the good news of forgiveness in Christ, people should be able to see His radiance in us—through our good works, through our attitudes when we're faced with trials, and through our love.

May we never keep Christ's light hidden, for that divine shine is most beautiful to behold!

Dear Lord, please let me be Your light in a
world that needs to find their way. Amen.—AH

GOD DAZZLES US ALL

The God of gods—it's GOD!—speaks out, shouts, "Earth!"
welcomes the sun in the east, farewells the disappearing
sun in the west. From the dazzle of Zion, God blazes into
view. Our God makes his entrance, he's not shy in his
coming. Starbursts of fireworks precede him.
PSALM 50:2–3 MSG

We live in a society that expects plenty of wow factor. In books, music, houses, art, clothing, architecture, movies, technology, everything really. If you can't present any dazzle, then step out of the game. Well, God is the master of dazzle in every way—in His spectacular creation, His supernatural miracles, His redemptive power, and His unfailing love. With all this dazzle astonishing us daily, why do we wake up yawning? People get bored too easily and forget too quickly.

Maybe we need to spend more time looking up. Perhaps we've been plodding along on a familiar footpath that we've created for ourselves because it's comfortable, and we've forgotten the wild and wonder-filled adventure that has been offered. As followers of Christ, we are redeemed, and we've been set on a journey that is not to be missed. Let us awaken spiritually so that the great adventure can begin!

Lord, sometimes I get so bogged down in my earthly existence
that I forget how to really live as You would want me to. You are
such a dazzling God. Help me to wake up spiritually! Amen.—AH

EVERY LITTLE DETAIL

But God, with the unfathomable richness of His love and mercy focused on us, united us with the Anointed One and infused our lifeless souls with life—even though we were buried under mountains of sin—and saved us by His grace.
Ephesians 2:4–5 voice

Parents love the details of their child's life. They record baby's first tooth, first solid foods, first words, first step, first haircut. . .well, first everything. Their child is the most beautiful kid ever born. The most precious. The most intelligent and creative. The most amazing person ever created. Why? Because their baby is their treasure. Yep, that's being a parent.

Hard to believe, but God loves us even more. Not in a standoffish, custodian-of-the-cosmos kind of way that sweeps through the ages. God loves each of us in a profoundly personal way. Even down to the very hairs on our heads. Luke 12:6-7 (NIV) says it almost lyrically: "Are not five sparrows sold for two pennies? Yet not one of them is forgotten by God. Indeed, the very hairs of your head are all numbered. Don't be afraid; you are worth more than many sparrows."

Lord Jesus, thank You for loving every detail of my life. I am so grateful for everything You've given me—the mercy, the forgiveness, and the eternal life! Amen.—AH

TRAVELER'S MALAISE
OF THE SOUL

"For God so loved the world, that he gave his only Son, that whoever believes in him should not perish but have eternal life."

JOHN 3:16 ESV

Have you ever been on a trip when you came down with something called traveler's malaise? Going through life in general can sometimes give us something similar—maybe we could call it a traveler's malaise of the soul. As Christians, we are merely traveling through this world. It is not our permanent home. We are sojourners on our way to a far better land. So, in a way, we will never feel quite at home here. But when that unsettled feeling turns into fear, could it come from having doubts about our salvation? At some point, we must take God at His word. John 3:16 expresses the promise of eternal life simply and perfectly and soundly.

We can accept this gift freely, and we can indeed know who we belong to and where we will be spending all of eternity. God really means it. We don't need to suffer from a traveler's malaise of the soul. We can be at peace. We can rejoice.

Lord, I praise You for giving me the assurance of salvation so I might go out into the world with confidence! Amen.—AH

MORE TIME FOR LOVE

"Do not seek revenge or bear a grudge against anyone among your people, but love your neighbor as yourself. I am the LORD."

LEVITICUS 19:18 NIV

People often complain that they never have enough hours in the day to fulfill their purpose in life, and yet we waste loads of time in the silliest and saddest ways. We basically don't act like the forgiven and blessed and creative people of God. If we embraced all that the Lord has given us, then we could let go of unforgiveness, slander, gossip, doubts, grudges, sinning, complaining, and obsessing—to name a few.

If we did walk away from these unsavory behaviors, think of all the extra hours we'd have, reaching for the dreams God has given us. And all the people we could tell about the Good News. And all the good we could do for people who are in need. And all the time we could spend communing with the Lord. And all the maturing we could do as women, and all the love we could share. Imagine. The world would become a much more lovable, breathable, livable world!

Mighty God, I want a fuller, freer life so that I will have more time to spend with You and more time to be all that You created me to be! In Jesus' powerful name I pray. Amen.—AH

LEAD WITH YOUR EARS

Post this at all the intersections, dear friends: Lead with your ears, follow up with your tongue, and let anger straggle along in the rear. God's righteousness doesn't grow from human anger. So throw all spoiled virtue and cancerous evil in the garbage. In simple humility, let our gardener, God, landscape you with the Word, making a salvation-garden of your life.
JAMES 1:19–21 MSG

A young woman named Judith had become known for blasting into a room with her mouth blazing with yak. She could fill the air with twittering chatter faster than an overcrowded aviary. Judith could outgab, outgossip, and outgrill anyone. It was a sight to behold, except many folks tended to miss it, since they were smart enough to run the other way. If you did brave one of Judith's chin-wagging sessions, and if you happened to set her off, oh dear. Prepare yourself for a sizable kaboom!

The book of James has some good commonsense ideas for dealing with these human frailties. Talking nonstop is not as good as being a gifted listener, and having a quick temper is not a good way to mature as a Christian. May we all pray for (and forgive) all the "Judiths" out there—even when that Judith is you or me.

Dear Lord, please show me how to lead with my ears instead of my big mouth! Amen.—AH

ABOUT THE GOOD SHEPHERD

*Jesus (with another parable): Wouldn't every single one
of you, if you have 100 sheep and lose one, leave the 99 in
their grazing lands and go out searching for the lost sheep
until you find it? When you find the lost sheep, wouldn't you
hoist it up on your shoulders, feeling wonderful? And when
you go home, wouldn't you call together your friends and
neighbors? Wouldn't you say, "Come over and celebrate
with me, because I've found my lost sheep"?*
LUKE 15:3–6 VOICE

Mirabella owned a small gallery, and she never ceased to be amazed by how often customers would request paintings that included a flock of sheep. She thought it might be that the sheep were so peaceful looking, or that the settings were usually serene. But as Mirabella reflected more on the matter, she realized these paintings had a beguiling connection to Jesus, the Good Shepherd. Even if people weren't Christ followers, they might be drawn to this distinctive art. Could it be that the pastoral image of sheep stirred up a soul longing? After all, who doesn't want to be found when they have been altogether lost? Who wouldn't want to have all the bad they've done in their lives washed clean away? Who wouldn't want to live for all time with the Maker of all beauty and joy and love?

Who indeed?

*Dearest Lord, Jesus, come be our Good Shepherd.
Our world is so very lost without You. Amen.–AH*

DANCING BEFORE GOD

And David danced before the Lord with all his might.
And David was wearing a linen ephod. So David and all the
house of Israel brought up the ark of the Lord with shouting
and with the sound of the horn. As the ark of the Lord came
into the city of David, Michal the daughter of Saul looked out
of the window and saw King David leaping and dancing
before the Lord, and she despised him in her heart.

2 Samuel 6:14–16 ESV

When we fall in love with the Lord, there's no telling what we might do to celebrate that extraordinary relationship. We might jump or shout or even dance before God like King David. We might sing a new song. We might write Him a love note or a poem, celebrating our forgiveness. We might build a little garden memorial to thank the Lord for His mercy and grace. Yes, we might do any number of things to show our thankfulness and create fellowship.

Does that mean we're being nonsensical or appalling or spinning out of control? No. Turn on the evening news, and you will see clearly what nonsensical and appalling and spinning out of control really look like! If people laugh at us for loving the Lord with all our hearts and souls–let them. In the end, it matters not what others think. It matters only what God thinks.

Lord, I love You so much! May our relationship
grow ever sweeter as time goes by. Amen.–AH

LIVING FREE AND FORGIVEN

God will wipe away every tear from their eyes; and death shall be no more, neither shall there be anguish (sorrow and mourning) nor grief nor pain any more, for the old conditions and the former order of things have passed away.

REVELATION 21:4 AMPC

Jillian was in a hurry and late for a meeting, so when she noticed the funeral procession, she groaned, knowing she would be even later. But wanting to do the right thing, she pulled over to the side of the road and stopped out of respect for the family and their loss. As the hearse motored by ever so slowly, Jillian felt a tinge of despair at the sight. To think that a person could be whirling through life and then suddenly be confronted with "that particular black car"—well, the realization would stop anyone cold.

And yet, as a Christian, Jillian reminded herself that the promises of God would hold true even to the end. That she had eternity to look forward to. Yes, living free and forgiven in Christ meant seeing death in a different light—in the light of heaven!

Dear Jesus, my Lord and Savior, I am grateful that because of Your work on the cross, death has lost its sting! I am looking forward to being with You in heaven! Amen.—AH

EMPTIED OUT

In your relationships with one another, have the same mindset as Christ Jesus: Who, being in very nature God, did not consider equality with God something to be used to his own advantage; rather, he made himself nothing by taking the very nature of a servant, being made in human likeness. And being found in appearance as a man, he humbled himself by becoming obedient to death—even death on a cross!

PHILIPPIANS 2:5–8 NIV

Moms tend to be mama bear-like when it comes to their kids, and if you mess with their cubs, well, be ready for a great hullabaloo. Along with that protectiveness is a stream of love that makes them want to empty themselves out for their kids all through their lives. That "emptying" may come in many forms, such as breastfeeding, prayer, help, thousands of meals, caregiving, financial assistance, more prayer, and—if we are truly honest—some handwringing. Were all these amazing gifts from Mom's hands and heart always appreciated? No. Sometimes the gifts were snatched up with barely an acknowledgment. But moms keep giving. . . .

That is the nature of God. He sent His Son, Jesus, who emptied Himself for us in many ways, including losing His very life for us. Have we thanked our Lord for the greatest gift of all?

Lord, thank You for emptying Yourself out for humanity—and for me. Amen.—AH

THE GIFT OF FORGIVENESS

*Then Peter came to Jesus and asked, "Lord, how
many times shall I forgive my brother or sister who
sins against me? Up to seven times?" Jesus answered,
"I tell you, not seven times, but seventy-seven times."*
MATTHEW 18:21–22 NIV

In this very broken world, the Lord knows there's going to be trouble. Jesus even told us that would be true. For instance, you get a group of people together for a meeting, and before you know it, a few 'tudes surface, and an atmosphere forms. Unfortunately, given enough time, the general "air" in the room may distill down into the tang of something akin to manure!

So what's next? Should we keep on forgiving and forgiving people? Yep, that is what the Lord says. Will we need the supernatural power of Christ to do it? Yes. Okay, but what if the other person never bothers to apologize, and it's clearly his or her fault? Well, give that problem to God. What if we can't seem to get the person's offense out of our heads and hearts? Give that angst to God too. The point is, we are in need of the Lord every minute of every day—for strength, for breath, for life, and yes, even for giving the gift of forgiveness.

*Lord, help me to forgive _____ for her sins against me.
I can't do this on my own. Please help me. And thank You
for forgiving all my many offenses! Amen.—AH*

ONLY A HEARTBEAT AWAY

When Jacob awoke from his sleep, he thought, "Surely the Lord is in this place, and I was not aware of it." He was afraid and said, "How awesome is this place! This is none other than the house of God; this is the gate of heaven."

GENESIS 28:16–17 NIV

When we come to know Christ as our Savior, there is merriment in heaven. Wouldn't you love to get a peek at that kind of celebration? Imagine a hallelujah chorus of angels on a grand and galactic scale!

As Christ followers, we can imagine that we, like Jacob, are waiting very near the gate of heaven. Only a thin veil separates us from this invisible realm. Since we are so near that house of God, we should think about the glorious way of life there. The divine details, so to speak. We know there will be no petty-mindedness, misunderstandings, or bitterness. No more bickering, unforgiveness, or grudges. There will be no more stains of life or sorrows of the soul. What there *will* be is beauty, light, creativity, purpose, fellowship, love—and more time than we can comprehend. Doesn't that truth make your spirit soar? Doesn't it stir your soul to want to live closer to the beautiful ways of God right now?

Lord, please help me to live out Your heavenly ideals right here on earth! Amen.—AH

THE TRUTH IN LOVE

"Stand up in the presence of the elderly, and show respect for the aged. Fear your God. I am the LORD."
LEVITICUS 19:32 NLT

Forgiving others is an important part of the Christian life. However, if some people display ongoing abusive conduct, you may need to set reasonable boundaries, walk away for a time, or even sever ties. Ask the Holy Spirit how He wants you to handle each situation, since there are as many unique scenarios as there are people!

For instance, younger people—according to the Bible—are to treat their elders with respect. Our society has gotten away from that precept to some degree, but it's still in the Word of God. Even though we are to forgive offenses—even rude actions—we do not have to remain silent. Ephesians 4:15 (NIV) reminds us, "Speaking the truth in love, we will grow to become in every respect the mature body of him who is the head, that is, Christ." In the end, speaking the truth in love is good for everyone.

So yes, forgive as Christ has forgiven us, but realize that silence does not always go hand in hand with mercy.

Father God, please help me to forgive people who have been hurtful to me. But also show me when I need to set reasonable boundaries and when I need to speak up. In Jesus' name I pray. Amen.—AH

THE SWEETEST SOUND

One of the criminals who were hanged railed at him, saying,
"Are you not the Christ? Save yourself and us!" But the other
rebuked him, saying, "Do you not fear God, since you are under
the same sentence of condemnation? And we indeed justly, for
we are receiving the due reward of our deeds; but this man has
done nothing wrong." And he said, "Jesus, remember me when
you come into your kingdom." And he said to him, "Truly, I say
to you, today you will be with me in paradise."
LUKE 23:39–43 ESV

On the day of Jesus' crucifixion, the two men who hung alongside Him, were thieves. They surely hoped they would escape their crimes, but now they were getting their due reward. When the two thieves came to realize that the man next to them was the Christ, they had a decision to make. One criminal was concerned about an earthly freedom, avoiding justice, but the other thief had a remorseful heart and wanted to be with the Lord in His kingdom. Jesus spoke to the second thief, and His words must have been the sweetest, most liberating utterances the man had ever heard. "Today you will be with me in paradise." From hopelessness to eternal life. One moment. One decision. And it would make a difference forever.

Everyone has a choice to make about Jesus. What is yours?

Lord, thank You for Your saving grace! Amen.–AH

ALL THE BRUNHILDAS

Be gentle and ready to forgive; never hold grudges.
Remember, the Lord forgave you, so you must forgive others.
COLOSSIANS 3:13 TLB

Luann knew she had been forgiven by the Lord, so she wanted to forgive others. Sounded like a win-win. *Bring it on, God!* she thought. On the way to drop off her child at school, Luann's dumpling darling gave her a shrug instead of a goodbye kiss. Okay, Luann could forgive that. Done. Then one of the school crossing guards came barreling toward Luann, giving her the evil eye. Maybe she could speed off, squealing her tires. But alas, too late. The woman leaned into Luann's open window, and for one dark second she considered rolling it up on her fingers. The woman was a Brunhilda type and a real thorn in her flesh!

Rats, Luann thought, *I could live an exemplary Christian life if it weren't for that one woman. What is God up to? Maybe Brunhilda was put in my life to teach me patience or how to take forgiveness to a higher level. Or maybe how to hide better. Just kidding, God.*

There's no doubt about it, though. Showing grace to the Brunhildas of this world requires a lot more prayer. No, forgiveness isn't easy, but it is always beautiful.

Lord, thanks for reminding me to pray for all those who
cross my path, especially the Brunhildas. Amen.—AH

AS FRESHLY FALLEN SNOW

*Come, let's talk this over, says the Lord; no matter how
deep the stain of your sins, I can take it out and make
you as clean as freshly fallen snow. Even if you are stained
as red as crimson, I can make you white as wool!*

ISAIAH 1:18 TLB

The landscape had taken on that bleak starkness of winter. The fields were a dozen shades of brown. Meadows once alive with grasses and blossoms and butterflies had all gone into a deep sleep. All that was left were remembrances of summer and the shadows of a past season.

But just when it seems winter holds no glimmer of glory or any radiance of hope, then comes the beauty of freshly falling snow, floating down lightly, flake upon flake, until all that was once dark and dirty is now white and pure. Miraculously, all has been covered in beauty!

That is the promise we cling to as Christians—that in Christ we are truly forgiven, and the bleak landscape of our sins has been transformed into pure white wonder.

All we have to do is ask.

*Lord Jesus, please forgive me for my transgressions.
I am going to trust that You will indeed make my
sins as white and pure as snow! Amen.—AH*

BREAKING GOD'S HEART

The Lord saw that the wickedness of man was great in the earth, and that every imagination and intention of all human thinking was only evil continually. And the Lord regretted that He had made man on the earth, and He was grieved at heart.
GENESIS 6:5–6 AMPC

After God created mankind, they fell into rebellion against the very hand that had loved them into existence. They continued to spiral into more and more wickedness until they were constantly doing evil. After Noah's flood with its accompanying judgment, humans still found themselves defying their Maker. Even in the midst of people's ongoing sin, Christ was sent to redeem us.

As Christians—even though we are forgiven and set free from the bondages of sin—we still at times find ourselves attempting various spiritual revolts. Doesn't seem possible? Too theatrical sounding? Well, every time we romance even the smallest sin, we step into the shadows—away from Christ's glorious light and presence. And in that stepping away, further and further, we must once again be breaking His heart. What a sad thought—and if we aren't sad, we should be!

May we choose every day, every hour, to stay out of the shadows and move ever closer to His sublime light and loving presence.

Lord, I feel sad thinking of the many ways I bring You sorrow. Please give me the power to please You and to bring You delight. Amen.—AH

JUST SOMETHING ABOUT HER

I can do all things [which He has called me to do] through Him
who strengthens and empowers me [to fulfill His purpose—
I am self-sufficient in Christ's sufficiency; I am ready for
anything and equal to anything through Him who infuses
me with inner strength and confident peace.]
PHILIPPIANS 4:13 AMP

If ever a woman could float, it was Miranda. She could put a swan to shame the way she glided across a room with silky grace. Her inner strength and peace were enviable, and if that wasn't enough, she even laughed in a musical sort of way. Basically, every woman wanted to be just like her.

Okay, so what was Miranda's secret? The woman had learned long ago that a great life in Christ meant she should simply take Him at His word. If the Lord said He was sufficient, He meant it. If the Lord said Miranda could do all things through Him, she would believe it. Took the stress right out of life. That new way of living was so freeing, Miranda now had more time to listen and love and laugh and truly live.

Yes, God had made a good plan, and Miranda intended to follow it with all her heart.

Lord, teach me how to take You at Your
word and live a freer life! Amen.—AH

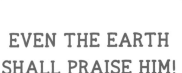

EVEN THE EARTH
SHALL PRAISE HIM!

*Let the heavens be glad, the earth rejoice; let the vastness
of the roaring seas demonstrate his glory. Praise him
for the growing fields, for they display his greatness.
Let the trees of the forest rustle with praise.*

PSALM 96:11–12 TLB

Every morning, Veronica sat in her breakfast nook sipping her coffee, and each morning she noticed a cute birdie fly down from the woods and perch on the top of her garden trellis. The bird would puff out her tiny chest, raise her beak to the heavens, and then sing her little heart out.

Also in Veronica's garden by the window, the flowers stretched their smiling faces toward the sun, and the trees rustled their leaves as if clapping their hands in an attitude of praise. There certainly seemed to be a glorious jubilee going on in God's creation!

How about us? Are we raising our little beaks and singing our hearts out to God?

*Mighty Creator God, I love all that You have made, for it is good
and glorious. Please remind me to wake up each morning with a
heart of praise and thanksgiving, not only for Your creation but
for Your plan of redemption! I love You more than words can say.
In Jesus' holy and powerful name I pray. Amen.—AH*

THE TOY BOX

So, my very dear friends, don't get thrown off course.
Every desirable and beneficial gift comes out of heaven.
The gifts are rivers of light cascading down from the Father of
Light. There is nothing deceitful in God, nothing two-faced,
nothing fickle. He brought us to life using the true Word,
showing us off as the crown of all his creatures.
JAMES 1:17–18 MSG

No doubt about it—you give a kid a toy box full of gifts and goodies to play with, and there's bound to be some giddy glee. Especially when that child has had a birthday and all the toys are brand new. Yep, prepare yourself for big noise. Your darling is headed for some serious play!

God made us that way, to be fun-loving and ingenious and whimsical at times. But grown-ups can get so bogged down in life that they lose their sense of wonder. Basically, they think their toy box has been empty for years, so why bother taking a fun peek? But God offers us desirable and beneficial gifts every day. We simply forget how to look for them—how to be delighted and give delight.

So. . .what could be in your toy box today?

Lord, I want to become like a child in my simple
faith and in my gratefulness for all Your good gifts,
including the light-filled gift of salvation! Amen.—AH

KEEPING A RECORD OF WRONGS

Love is patient, love is kind. It does not envy, it does not boast,
it is not proud. It does not dishonor others, it is not self-seeking,
it is not easily angered, it keeps no record of wrongs.

1 CORINTHIANS 13:4–5 NIV

June shuffled through her pile of lists and had to admit that keeping up with all the ways people had offended her was getting complicated and time-consuming, not to mention exhausting! June had lists of wrongdoings for family members, friends, and people at work. She even had a list for acquaintances. But when June stared at the sweaty little lists, which had been scrawled out in haste and anger, she paused.

What had God said about keeping a record of wrongs? Hmm. June flipped her Bible over to 1 Corinthians 13 and read the whole love chapter. She sighed. How had she forgotten such a simple and beautiful precept? Then God reminded her of all the many ways He had graciously forgiven her time and time again.

Suddenly those lists no longer looked like valuable records worth keeping but more like trash. So June tossed all the lists and called up one of her friends for lunch. It was going to be a good day. . . .

Lord Jesus, I admit I tend to keep a record of wrongs
on people. I am truly sorry for this. Help me to
forgive others as You forgive me. Amen.–AH

GENEROUS FOLK

"For if you give, you will get! Your gift will return to you in full and overflowing measure, pressed down, shaken together to make room for more, and running over. Whatever measure you use to give—large or small—will be used to measure what is given back to you."

LUKE 6:38 TLB

The Magpie family had come from a long line of cheapskates and stingy folk. Sometimes this family of misers joked about it. Or even bragged about their tightfisted exploits! They were notorious, known far and wide as a nest of squirrels.

But through the years, other people who had been on the receiving end of the Magpies' miserliness, well, they weren't laughing. The workers who were employed by the Magpies had never received a decent wage. Service providers never saw a tip come from their hand. And forget about Christmas with a little something extra in your stocking. This family could have tutored Scrooge!

Then there is generosity. Luke 6:38 sure has a few things to say about that.

How do we want to be remembered in this life? Known far and wide as a nest of squirrels? Or as generous folk who loved big, forgave easily, and gave lavishly!

Dear Lord, show me how to have a charitable heart like Yours, for You are a generous God. Amen.—AH

LIVING A LIFE OF DENIAL

If we say (claim) we have not sinned, we contradict His Word and make Him out to be false and a liar, and His Word is not in us [the divine message of the Gospel is not in our hearts].

1 JOHN 1:10 AMPC

People put a ton of energy into making other people believe something about them that may or may not be true. We parade around wearing various got-my-act-together masks, and we don't take them off until we get home—and sometimes not even then. We get proficient at denying our pain, our past, our fears, our doubts, and most everything else. Worst of all, we sometimes get caught denying that we're sinners.

We pour so much effort and energy into living a life of denial. Honestly, if we would put even half as much effort into simply confessing our sins to Christ with a sincere heart, we sure would experience a happier world down here!

Can I get an amen, sister?

Lord God, I know I am a sinner. Forgive me for _____. Please help me not to fall into that transgression again. Thank You for Your patience with me as I grow up as a believer. I want to please You in all I do. In Jesus' powerful and holy name I pray. Amen.—AH

A STRANGE MADNESS

This is the One who—imprinted with God's image, shimmering
with His glory—sustains all that exists through the power of His
word. He was seated at the right hand of God once He Himself
had made the offering that purified us from all our sins.
HEBREWS 1:3 VOICE

If you ever open a box stuffed full of those teeny-tiny Styrofoam packing fragments, and they escape, you're in for a wild ride. As you try to sweep up the fluffy bits, they whirl off and scatter everywhere. They won't stay put, so you feel as though you're sweeping air. After a while, the scene morphs into a strange sort of madness. You want to give up.

That scenario is a little like trying to find a way to live in this world without God's help. We run around wildly doing this and that, wearing ourselves out, and then we become as unproductive and silly as a person sweeping the air. In the end, our efforts will do no good and become a strange sort of madness.

Bottom line? We need God. I need God. You need God. 'Nuff said.

Lord Jesus, I need You every hour of every day. I can't do this
by myself. Please guide and direct me always. Amen.–AH

IT WAS PURE LOVE

*Let your heart overflow with praise to the True
God of heaven, for His faithful love lasts forever.*
PSALM 136:26 VOICE

Imagine this—large black wings are making monstrous-looking shadows over your house, and when you look up through a window, you can see the vultures are circling. You step out of the house, and the stench of something foul stings your nostrils. You back away, wanting to hurry back inside. You know an animal has died and the vultures are taking care of business. For some reason, even though death is part of our human existence, you hate it. Why does everything have to end like this? Birth, growth, and then death? What can it all mean? It's disgusting and sad and almost unbearable. Why? These are questions that mankind has been asking since the fall in the Garden of Eden.

The story is so simple but so tragic. There was a garden. There was a couple. And there was a God who loved them beyond anything imaginable. But the people decided it just wasn't enough. And so death was born.

Then that same God—who loved us beyond anything imaginable—decided that redemption was the only way. It was pure love—once again. Surely now we are wise enough to choose love. . . .

*Lord Jesus, I choose You and Your
love every time! Amen.—AH*

I AM AT THE DOOR

"Look! I have been standing at the door, and I am constantly knocking. If anyone hears me calling him and opens the door, I will come in and fellowship with him and he with me."
REVELATION 3:20 TLB

The mother sat on the bus, riding home. She slipped on her sunglasses so no one could see her as she wept softly. She had shed a thousand tears for her wayward daughter and had said just as many prayers. Today, she'd traveled to her daughter's apartment to give her a large amount of money—cash her daughter had said she desperately needed. Just when she thought her daughter might invite her in for a cup of tea and a visit, instead, she slowly closed the door in her face.

That day, the mother's heart broke, but she would never stop loving her daughter, no matter what. She cried out to the Lord in her helplessness. Somehow, there on that smelly old bus, God came close and lifted her spirit.

God loves us—no matter what. The Lord has given us—His wayward sons and daughters—every kind of blessing. Mercy, forgiveness, grace, hope, joy, purpose, love—everything. He is knocking and wants to come in to fellowship. Not just to give us things, but to be with us. May we always open the door to our families and to our God.

Lord, thank You for all Your blessings and for the gift of Your fellowship. Amen.—AH

A FRAGRANT OFFERING

Follow God's example, therefore, as dearly loved children and walk in the way of love, just as Christ loved us and gave himself up for us as a fragrant offering and sacrifice to God.

EPHESIANS 5:1–2 NIV

The Bible mentions oils, herbs, and perfumes numerous times. It becomes obvious that God loves a great perfume! After all, He created the resources and the expertise for people to make them. In recent times, people have enjoyed these natural essences more and more. In fact, these beneficial oils have become a huge industry.

The Bible goes beyond just the mention of these wonderful gifts. The Word of God instructs us to live a life that is a pleasing fragrance. How do we do that? By walking in the way of love. Uh-oh. That sounds pretty close to impossible in this broken world. Yes, it is. But we can accomplish all kinds of things with Christ's supernatural help. With Jesus in our hearts, we can give off an irresistible fragrance of divine love wherever we go—to please God, to bring us joy, and to point others toward Christ's redemptive grace.

Mighty God, please help me to swirl through this life giving off Your exquisite scent of love everywhere I go. In Jesus' powerful name I pray. Amen.—AH

HAVE WE LOST OUR MINDS?

"You will be driven away from people and will live with the wild animals; you will eat grass like the ox. Seven times will pass by for you until you acknowledge that the Most High is sovereign over all kingdoms on earth and gives them to anyone he wishes." Immediately what had been said about Nebuchadnezzar was fulfilled. He was driven away from people and ate grass like the ox. His body was drenched with the dew of heaven until his hair grew like the feathers of an eagle and his nails like the claws of a bird.

DANIEL 4:32–33 NIV

When you watch the evening news, do you ever get the idea that our nation—and world—has lost its collective mind? We have lost our way because, like King Nebuchadnezzar, we've become spiritually arrogant, turning away from the one true King of kings. As a result, humanity sometimes acts as insane as Nebuchadnezzar when he was eating grass like an ox!

Fortunately for Nebuchadnezzar, he realized his foolishness, and his sanity returned to him. This passage goes on to read, "At the end of that time, I, Nebuchadnezzar, raised my eyes toward heaven, and my sanity was restored. Then I praised the Most High; I honored and glorified him who lives forever" Daniel 4:34 (NIV). May our world come to know the one true God!

Lord, may our nation and our world lift their eyes up toward heaven and seek You and Your redemption! Amen.—AH

WE ARE ALL GOD'S FAVORITES

It makes no difference to me (or to God for that matter)
if people have power or influence. God doesn't choose
favorites among His children. Even the so-called pillars
of the church didn't contribute anything new to
my understanding of the good news.

GALATIANS 2:6 VOICE

Darcia mingled with the other partygoers, having a nice time for a change, so grateful that no one had taken notice yet of who she was. Usually as soon as people recognized her from the popular TV series, well, everyone changed. Right now, people were cordial. People were real. But at any moment there could be a gasping and then a hovering. People would turn fake and act way beyond cordial. Darcia admitted that the fame had its upsides, but the downside was that too often people would become extra friendly because they wanted something from her. Sometimes people would even claim they'd move heaven and earth for her. What a joke, because when they thought Darcia was an ordinary person, she couldn't even get them to move her couch!

Fortunately, God never treats us this way. He plays no favorites, treating us all the same. God loves everyone, and His message of salvation is for all.

Lord, thank You that You are no
respecter of persons! Amen.–AH

HELP MY UNBELIEF!

"And the demon often makes him fall into the fire or into water to kill him. Oh, have mercy on us and do something if you can." "If I can?" Jesus asked. "Anything is possible if you have faith." The father instantly replied, "I do have faith; oh, help me to have more!" When Jesus saw the crowd was growing, he rebuked the demon. "O demon of deafness and dumbness," he said, "I command you to come out of this child and enter him no more!"

MARK 9:22–25 TLB

People toss around the word *faith* like spiritual confetti. They say, "You need it. You can't live without it. Pray for it. Grow it. Use it." But sometimes when life throws you a major trial, you might find yourself wallowing in tremendous guilt because doubt has come for an unwelcome visit. Then you have to deal with the trial, plus the guilt and doubt! But as humans we will always struggle with bits or even boulders of doubt. The man in this Bible passage had some faith, but Jesus encouraged him to have more. Then the man appeared to take a leap of faith by asking for more. Jesus followed through by miraculously healing his son from a demon.

So when doubts do come for a visit, never hesitate to boldly ask the Lord for more faith. He will never answer your prayer with anger but rather with love.

Lord, I want to believe. Please help me to overcome my doubts! Amen.—AH

GONE MISSING?

*And while they were there, the time came for her to
give birth. And she gave birth to her firstborn son and
wrapped him in swaddling cloths and laid him in a manger,
because there was no place for them in the inn.*

LUKE 2:6–7 ESV

Come every Christmas season, churches all over the globe recognize the birth of Christ, and sometimes they recreate a manger scene to help remind the world why we celebrate and Who we worship. But what if, across the world, all the baby Jesuses suddenly disappeared? What if people walked up to the mangers and found them empty? What if the nativity story became only a distant memory? Perhaps just a fond fable told during the holidays? How easy would it be to forget what's important, *who* is important, and why Jesus came?

Perhaps our world is already moving from faith to fable.

Isaiah 9:6 (VOICE) says it beautifully: "Hope of all hopes, dream of our dreams, a child is born, sweet-breathed; a son is given to us: a living gift. And even now, with tiny features and dewy hair, He is great. The power of leadership, and the weight of authority, will rest on His shoulders. His name? His name we'll know in many ways—He will be called Wonderful Counselor, Mighty God, Dear Father everlasting, ever-present never-failing, Master of Wholeness, Prince of Peace."

*Lord, may I never forget the glorious
"Who" of Christmas! Amen.—AH*

FATHER, FORGIVE THEM

*And when they came to the place that is called The Skull,
there they crucified him, and the criminals, one on his right
and one on his left. And Jesus said, "Father, forgive them,
for they know not what they do." And they cast lots to divide
his garments. And the people stood by, watching, but the
rulers scoffed at him, saying, "He saved others; let him
save himself, if he is the Christ of God, his Chosen One!"*

LUKE 23:33–35 ESV

If you have lived on this planet for any length of time, you have come to know rejection. It might come in the form of a tiny snub, or it can be an all-out rejection that causes tremendous heartache.

Yet no one can truly comprehend the anguish of the Messiah, who willingly offered Himself to be tortured and to die a most excruciating death for the redemption of mankind—all in the name of love.

In the midst of this anguish that humans placed on Christ, our Lord said the most tender and loving words this world could ever know. "Father, forgive these people. They don't know what they are doing."

Friends, this means that suffering has turned into triumph, death into life, sin into pardon. May our souls grab hold of this Good News with gusto!

*Lord, praise You and thank You for Your
glorious gift of grace! Amen.—AH*

OUR SPLENDOR

*"I adorned you with jewelry: I put bracelets on your arms and
a necklace around your neck, and I put a ring on your nose,
earrings on your ears and a beautiful crown on your head.
So you were adorned with gold and silver; your clothes were
of fine linen and costly fabric and embroidered cloth. Your
food was honey, olive oil and the finest flour. You became
very beautiful and rose to be a queen. And your fame spread
among the nations on account of your beauty, because the
splendor I had given you made your beauty perfect, declares
the Sovereign LORD. But you trusted in your beauty and used
your fame to become a prostitute. You lavished your favors
on anyone who passed by and your beauty became his."*
EZEKIEL 16:11–15 NIV

Even though these verses are referring to the Jewish nation, they are of great value even today. May we ask ourselves how we treat this God-man who redeemed us—Jesus Christ—who gave us every kind of blessing. Yes, the beauty of grace and mercy, peace and joy, forgiveness and love. How have we responded? Do we take our God-given splendor and use it for unseemly purposes? Do we use our talents for the sole purpose of our own glory, or for His? Do we thank our dear Lord for all that He has given us? God deserves our love, for He is the author of love.

Jesus, may I never stray from Your love! Amen.—AH

PREPARE TO BE WOWED

And the twelve gates were twelve pearls, each of the gates made of a single pearl, and the street of the city was pure gold, like transparent glass. And I saw no temple in the city, for its temple is the Lord God the Almighty and the Lamb. And the city has no need of sun or moon to shine on it, for the glory of God gives it light, and its lamp is the Lamb. By its light will the nations walk, and the kings of the "earth will bring their glory into it, and its gates will never be shut by day—and there will be no night there.
REVELATION 21:21–25 ESV

People are attracted to beauty in all its forms—the spectacular display of God's creation, songs that stir us deep in our souls, a newborn babe caressing your cheek with velvety fingers. Everything that has real beauty is either made by God or the result of the resources, talent, and creativity He has provided. Christ promised us that He is preparing a glorious place for all who love Him and follow Him. If you think the earth has a lot of wow factor, then just imagine what heaven will be like! No one will be disappointed when they arrive. No one.

Lord Jesus, thank You for Your redeeming grace enabling me to enter the gates of heaven one day! Amen.—AH

WHEN I STEP AWAY

*But for me it is good to be near God; I have made
the Lord GOD my refuge, that I may tell of all your works.*
PSALM 73:28 ESV

We humans are full of oddities. One peculiarity is that we may say we love God, but our actions don't always reflect that assertion. When we stay near God, our souls thrive, so that even when hard times come, we can still sense the strong arms of the Lord sustaining us. But what happens when we do the opposite? When we know full well that we are straying outside of God's precepts and living by our own rules? Any number of things can go wrong. We can eventually lose our sense of right and wrong. We may come to see good as evil and evil as good.

As we fall away from God, we may begin to think the abyss is a fine place to be. And we might suffer with more doubts. More fear. More anger. More confusion. More rebellion against the one true God who loves steadfastly, forgives freely, and always wants the very best for us!

*Father God, may I never choose to step away from You,
even for a moment! Help me to remain steadfast in
my love for You. In Jesus' name I pray. Amen.–AH*

A DOUBLE LIFE

Come close to the one true God, and He will draw close to you. Wash your hands; you have dirtied them in sin. Cleanse your heart, because your mind is split down the middle, your love for God on one side and selfish pursuits on the other.
JAMES 4:8 VOICE

Many people could look at Paula and say, "What a fine specimen of Christian womanhood!" Yes, Paula really seemed to have her spiritual act together. But there was another side to her. Paula knew it. God knew it. And some people who were very close to her were beginning to see it. Paula led a double life. No, she wasn't concealing criminal activities, but she knew all too well that some of her motivations and feelings were offensive to God. She would give generously, but her charity was not without resentment. She would cheer someone on, but nurse some sizable envy too. She sang in the choir but for the applause of people, not for the glory of God.

Nobody goes to jail for these kinds of wrongs, and yet there is an imprisonment of the soul that goes along with them, not to mention the sorrow we cause the Holy Spirit! What can we do? We can confess that we live a double life. We can come close to God and let Him cleanse our hearts from all unrighteousness. Remember, forgiveness is merely a prayer away.

Lord, cleanse my heart in every way! Amen.—AH

A LOVE MOST SPLENDID

In him we have redemption through his
blood, the forgiveness of our trespasses,
according to the riches of his grace.
EPHESIANS 1:7 ESV

The cross of Christ is something that can be hard to talk about. Not just because the ancient form of crucifixion has a grisly and anguishing history connected to it, but also because the symbol of the cross represents our sin against God. People don't like to think about the S word. Too off-putting and too much guilt associated with it. We live in a society that wants to flee from any kind of guilt. The only problem is, we are all as guilty as sin.

The good news is that all of us are offered salvation and new life through Christ's redeeming blood, which He shed on that cross. Can we not also see the irresistible nature of this sacrifice? After all, it's about grace and forgiveness and freedom. It's about beauty and life and a love most splendid. If we're going to flee, may we flee into the arms of Christ's love.

Almighty God, I am deeply grateful to You for sending
Your Son, and I thank You that He paid the debt for my sins.
I am also profoundly happy that You've promised me the
gift of eternal life in heaven. In Jesus' name I pray. Amen.—AH

I LOVE YOU!

You are precious in my sight,
and honored, and I love you.
ISAIAH 43:4 NRSV

Zoe's mom had always been there for her, but she'd always done it in a distant way. She made sure Zoe had what she needed as she grew up, yet something was always missing. When her mom said she loved her, it was always after Zoe had said it first. And her mom always said the words in a generic, detached way. As if her mom was in love with mankind but not her exactly.

Then one night in her sleep, Zoe dreamed she was wandering through a garden, lonely and lost. Jesus walked up beside her, and they sat down together on a bench. They talked for a long time, about anything and everything. Then Jesus reached out to Zoe, took her face in the palms of His hands, and said the words her heart had so longed to hear: "I love you, Zoe." She burst into tears, not of pain, but of pure joy. Zoe woke up knowing she would remember that dream always, for she had met the most heartfelt and intimate and everlasting love in the world. A love that wasn't faraway or vague, but real and impassioned. The love of Christ.

Today, God says to me and to you, "I love you!"

Lord, thank You for Your healing word
to me. I love You too! Amen.–AH

HIDDEN THINGS

We have all become like one who is unclean, and all our
righteous deeds are like a polluted garment. We all fade
like a leaf, and our iniquities, like the wind, take us away.
ISAIAH 64:6 ESV

Luella noticed that the smell seeping out of the garbage can was beyond bearable. Her husband had forgotten to take it to the curb, so they would have to deal with a few more days of the smothering stench of trash in the summer heat. Oy! Then Luella got an idea. She had some perfume she no longer wore, so she opened the bottle and poured the sweet liquid all over the garbage. What a fix. Later, Luella went back out in the garage and winced. The perfume hadn't covered up the stench but had only compounded it!

And so it goes with our good deeds. In Isaiah we read, "All our righteous deeds are like a polluted garment." We think our deeds are noble, but many times something less noble is hidden behind them, such as motivations that are infused with self rather than service. Even as followers of Christ, we are ever in need of help, forgiveness, guidance, and encouragement. We are a needy people, so how wonderful it is that our Lord is a giving God!

Lord, when I do good works in Your name,
may I have a servant's heart. Amen.—AH

WHEN I FEEL JEALOUSY

*For you are still [unspiritual, having the nature] of the flesh
[under the control of ordinary impulses]. For as long as [there
are] envying and jealousy and wrangling and factions among
you, are you not unspiritual and of the flesh, behaving yourselves after a human standard and like mere (unchanged) men?*
1 CORINTHIANS 3:3 AMPC

Jealousy is a word that can generate tremendous emotion, and the
feeling of jealousy can be destructive, stressful, and all too familiar.
One scenario might be that you feel a terrible sadness when a lifelong
friend abandons you because she found a new friend who has more
appeal. After a lengthy friendship, an occurrence like this can be very
painful, and it is not wrong to feel sadness, acknowledge your hurt
feelings, and even speak to your friend about her abandonment in
love. But if your pain turns into jealousy and bitterness, you are bound
to face some spiritual trouble.

Throughout life, jealousy can be connected to other emotions,
such as resentment, insecurity, possessiveness, and even hatred. If you
are confused about your emotions, talk to God about them. He will be
pleased to help you sort out what is right and good and what is sin.

The bottom line is—the Lord doesn't want us to follow human stan-
dards but to live as transformed and confident women of God!

*Lord, I can't become a transformed and confident
woman on my own. Please help me! Amen.–AH*

WHEN I'M ANGRY

Good sense makes one slow to anger,
and it is his glory to overlook an offense.
PROVERBS 19:11 ESV

Have you ever known anyone—man or woman—who gets angry over almost anything? If she runs out of milk, she rants about who drank it all up. If she stubs her toe, she howls and squawks. Someone cuts ahead of her in line at the grocery store, and wow, she lets the woman have it with a few choice words. And you can bet none of those words are from Sunday morning worship! Working with or living with a person like this can be a painful ordeal. Or maybe living inside this person, in case that person is you!

Every day any number of things can get under our skin. That may be why the Bible instructs us to be slow to anger. It doesn't say we won't ever feel that way. Anger and frustration are inevitable in such a maddening, bewildering, and anguish-filled world. But when we do succumb to anger, it is right and good to let it go. And it is to our glory to overlook other people's offenses. These divine attitudes may not get the world's stamp of approval, but in the end they will please God and help us to live more poised, positive, and pleasant lives!

Lord, I admit I get angry easily. Please give me a
more mature and mellow disposition. Amen.—AH

WHAT IF?

"The son said to him, 'Father, I have sinned against heaven and against you. I am no longer worthy to be called your son.' But the father said to his servants, 'Quick! Bring the best robe and put it on him. Put a ring on his finger and sandals on his feet. Bring the fattened calf and kill it. Let's have a feast and celebrate. For this son of mine was dead and is alive again; he was lost and is found.' So they began to celebrate."
LUKE 15:21–24 NIV

The prodigal son is one of the most popular stories in the Bible. We weep for joy when the son comes to his senses and rushes home to what his heart had longed for all along—the presence of his father who loved him profoundly. But here's an odd addition to the story that could make us ponder it further. What if the prodigal son had wanted to come back home for all his father's goodies, but he didn't want to fully repent? What if the son had even wanted to bring his wayward friends home with him, hoping they could still live a bit wildly?

That twist ruins the story! But how many times have we messed up our life story by not being truly sorry or wanting to mend our willful ways? Christ's forgiveness is real, but our repentance needs to be real too.

Lord, when I sin, may I always have a repentant heart. Amen.—AH

AN UNEMPTY TOMB?

*Then Simon Peter came, following him, and went into
the tomb. He saw the linen cloths lying there, and the face
cloth, which had been on Jesus' head, not lying with the
linen cloths but folded up in a place by itself. Then the other
disciple, who had reached the tomb first, also went in, and
he saw and believed; for as yet they did not understand
the Scripture, that he must rise from the dead.*

JOHN 20:6–9 ESV

The greatest holidays in the world—Christmas and Easter—have meaning because the tomb of Christ was found empty. The Good News for mankind hangs on Christ's resurrection from the dead. If the tomb still held the bones of Jesus, there would be no hope for us. None. We would be a planet swirling in space for no reason at all. There would be life, yes—but lived out for what purpose? And with no life eternal, what genuine hope is there to be found?

But the stone was rolled away. The tomb was indeed found empty, and light flooded that space. Love won that day and for all time.

The empty tomb of Christ is a beautiful sign of God's love for us. We have been offered mercy, forgiveness, freedom, joy, peace, hope, and a most glorious future in heaven!

*Mighty God, thank You for sending Your Son
to conquer sin and death and for offering me
redemption. In Jesus' name I pray. Amen.—AH*

ILL-FITTING SHOES

For this world is not our permanent home;
we are looking forward to a home yet to come.
HEBREWS 13:14 NLT

You just got back from the mall, and you are so thrilled with your new shoes. They are chic to the max, and they make you look more youthful. But after that hefty walk all the way to your car in those new shoes, well, your bunions ache, your bone spur is screaming, and you are one breath away from driving right back to the store and demanding your money back. Then you remember that the sales clerk mentioned the shoes were leather and would loosen up after a while. Hmm. So you give it some time. Later on, those shoes do start to feel better, but you always feel a pinch or two.

Isn't life in this fallen world a lot like a pair of ill-fitting shoes that cause us pain? No matter how great a day or week might go for us, we will still feel the pinch of sin, the ploys of the enemy, and the daily affliction of living on a planet that's determined to be in rebellion against God.

So we shouldn't feel shocked that we don't seem to belong in this broken place. Hebrews reminds us that our home here is not permanent and that we can look forward to the world to come. Let us say amen to that!

Lord, thank You for forgiveness,
for reconciliation, for eternal life! Amen.—AH

I CAN'T DANCE ANY FASTER

*"Come to me and I will give you rest—all of you who work so
hard beneath a heavy yoke. Wear my yoke—for it fits perfectly—
and let me teach you; for I am gentle and humble, and you
shall find rest for your souls; for I give you only light burdens."*
MATTHEW 11:28 TLB

The poor dear woman, Emily, dropped onto the couch as she burst into
tears. She looked up to the heavens and said to God, "I can't dance
any faster."

So many demands had been piling up on Emily, at home and at
work, even at church. When it came to weariness in mind, body, and
spirit, she had come to the end of herself. Emily did right in approaching
the Lord with her problem. His loving arms were just the right place to
be. Jesus said it so beautifully—we are to allow Him to teach us, for He
is gentle and humble. He will give us rest for our souls, for He gives us
only burdens that are light.

Confidence returns when we know that we can lean on God—for
everything. We can stop our wild dance—that is, trying to be all things
to all people. It is not possible, and so instead we can rest and walk with
God, and even take time to play and laugh and love!

*Holy Spirit, show me how to live fully—
the way You want me to. Amen.—AH*

THE GREATEST OF SINNERS

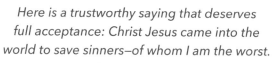

*Here is a trustworthy saying that deserves
full acceptance: Christ Jesus came into the
world to save sinners—of whom I am the worst.*
1 TIMOTHY 1:15 NIV

One of the occasions we humans tend to back away from God is when we get scared, thinking we've gone too far and sinned too much to ever come back home. Well, don't you believe it—those are lies of the enemy. Jesus didn't come to condemn anyone but rather to love each of us into the kingdom of God.

Anytime you think you've sinned too big, remember the apostle Paul. He called himself the worst sinner. And indeed, Paul was involved in some heinous activities, including persecuting the church and imprisoning the followers of Christ. And yet God used Paul in mighty ways for His glory. Paul helped change the course of history when he spread the Good News of Christ and when he wrote—through the power of the Holy Spirit—at least thirteen of the New Testament books. God had the power and love to transform wickedness into something wondrous. Paul is the proof, and so are we.

Forgiveness is for everyone, all the time. So let no one, let nothing, keep you from running back into the arms of the Lord. He is there, ever waiting for you, ever loving you.

*Lord, thank You for Your boundless
mercy and grace! Amen.—AH*

GOOD MEDICINE

A happy heart is good medicine
and a cheerful mind works healing,
but a broken spirit dries up the bones.
PROVERBS 17:22 AMPC

Tillie snapped off the evening news. She suddenly felt heavy in her shoulders, in her head, and worst of all, in her spirit. Such endless doom and gloom on the tube. Tillie then tuned in to a channel that featured Christian comedians. Okay, the gal was kind of funny, and Tillie felt a smile grace her lips. Then she sputtered out a tiny chortle. Before long, Tillie was busting out with laughter. Her shoulders relaxed, her head stopped pounding, and her spirit felt lighter.

People can't honestly say that life is a breeze. If they did say it, they would be liars! Yes, there may be breezy days and glorious moments that seem like glimpses into the heavenly realm, but life can be brutal too. One comfort to the soul is to cultivate a merry heart. People are used to taking tons of supplements and meds, so wouldn't it be wonderful to add this one? After all, the Bible calls a happy heart good medicine and says that a cheerful mind will work healing in us. God has already written the prescription. We just need to fill it!

Dearest Lord, please help me to find ways to get my sense of humor back. A merry heart will make me heathier, and it will make my witness to the world more winsome, confident, and appealing. Amen.–
AH

FORGETTING SOMEONE?

How can you disown your God like that? Can a girl forget her jewels? What bride will seek to hide her wedding dress? Yet for years on end my people have forgotten me—the most precious of their treasures.
JEREMIAH 2:32 TLB

Georgina loved her family dearly. When she realized they had no formal photo of them all together, she decided to pay for a big photo shoot. They all dressed in shades of ivory and tan so they'd be coordinated and beautiful. But the moment the photo shoot began, her kids and grandkids changed the agenda. They took one photo of Georgina at the back and then asked her to step out of the picture for the rest of the photo shoot. A flood of sadness filled her being, and tears threatened. She ran to the restroom to recover, but she couldn't quite do it. Georgina knew the truth—she had been forgotten.

That's a bit like what the Israelites did to God—even though the Lord was the One to bring them life and the One who loved them beyond anyone else. Some days, have we been caught treating God in the same way? Using Him for what He can give us, but when it comes to love and fellowship, asking Him to step out of the family photo?

Forgive me, Lord, for forgetting You sometimes.
You are my beloved, and I always want You
front and center in my life! Amen.—AH

GETTING TO KNOW HIM

*But grow in spiritual strength and become better acquainted
with our Lord and Savior Jesus Christ. To him be all glory
and splendid honor, both now and forevermore.*

2 PETER 3:18 TLB

Falling in love or getting to know someone can be a beautiful thing. Getting to know our kids better and better as they grow up, well, that can be a wonderful adventure too! Making a new friend can be satisfying and full of delights as well.

As Christians, since we are going to spend eternity with God, don't we want to get to know Him better and better as we read in 2 Peter? We can grow closer to the Lord through the power of the Holy Spirit, through inspired sermons and the fellowship of believers at church, through the Living Word of God, through heartening words from other Christ followers, through the glories of God's creation, through art and music and our own God-given talents, through prayer and time spent in the Lord's divine presence, and through anything else God wants to use for us to get to know Him better and better.

What a glorious pleasure when we can honestly say, "I so get You, God. . .and it is the greatest thing ever!"

*Oh Lord, I love spending time with You and getting
to know You better. You are marvelous! Amen.–AH*

SO MUCH TO BE SAID!

"This is how I want you to conduct yourself in these matters. If you enter your place of worship and, about to make an offering, you suddenly remember a grudge a friend has against you, abandon your offering, leave immediately, go to this friend and make things right. Then and only then, come back and work things out with God."
MATTHEW 5:23-24 MSG

We rush through life like whirling leaves in a sudden autumn gust. In the process of that whirling, we sometimes forget or refuse to say and do what needs to be said and done. So many times, we hear years later—through another person—that we were deeply appreciated for something we did. Or that so-and-so really bragged on our talents or enjoyed our gifts and kindnesses. Or perhaps we discovered through a third party that we were forgiven or admired or truly loved.

Why do we withhold what is good and godly? Are we too shy, too insensitive, too cowardly, too stubborn, or too prideful to walk up to the person and just say what should be said in love?

People long for heaven on earth. Well, here's one way to get started!

Holy Spirit, please give me the courage to speak the truth in love. I don't want to grieve You, but instead I want to make You proud. Amen.—AH

REAL VULNERABILITY

This is how we know what love is:
Jesus Christ laid down his life for us.
1 JOHN 3:16 NIV

After a nice lunch and a short drive home, Amy got a little angry. It seemed as though her gal friend had taken advantage of her pocketbook. When her friend told her she was short on cash, Amy felt obligated to pick up the check for lunch. Yet again.

We do tend to get a little pouty when we think we've been put into a weakened position or someone has taken advantage of us. But our complaints are nothing compared to the vulnerabilities that Christ knew on earth. After all, He came via the womb of a young woman, not riding down on fiery clouds in a golden chariot as He had every right to! Beyond Christ's helpless kind of entrance, He knew unfathomable suffering, loneliness, rejection, and torture.

Isaiah 53:3 (NIV) tells us, "He was despised and rejected by mankind, a man of suffering, and familiar with pain. Like one from whom people hide their faces he was despised, and we held him in low esteem." If that wasn't enough, Christ laid down His very life for us. What a striking picture of vulnerability!

Jesus, thank You for all You've done for me! Amen.—AH

JESUS CALLS IT GRACE

Even though we were dead because of our sins, he gave us life when he raised Christ from the dead. (It is only by God's grace that you have been saved!) For he raised us from the dead along with Christ and seated us with him in the heavenly realms because we are united with Christ Jesus. So God can point to us in all future ages as examples of the incredible wealth of his grace and kindness toward us, as shown in all he has done for us who are united with Christ Jesus.

EPHESIANS 2:5–7 NLT

When writers want to come up with a big idea in nonfiction, sometimes they will cook up five handy tips or a few easy ways to improve relationships or foster personal growth. These lists seem to make growth and maturity sound more doable, more approachable—because altering our lives is rarely easy.

When it comes to the biggest change a human soul can undergo, thank God—literally—that we only need one miraculous way to freedom. The world might call it impossible, but Jesus just calls it grace.

Lord God Almighty, I am so profoundly grateful You chose to send Your Son so that my soul could know the biggest, boldest, brightest change imaginable. I praise You now and forevermore. In Jesus' holy and powerful name I pray. Amen.—AH

BOBBLED OUT

"Do not store up for yourselves treasures on earth, where moths and vermin destroy, and where thieves break in and steal. But store up for yourselves treasures in heaven, where moths and vermin do not destroy, and where thieves do not break in and steal. For where your treasure is, there your heart will be also."
MATTHEW 6:19-21 NIV

If shopping were a sport, Jenny would be a champion! Yes, browsing and bargaining and buying had become paramount in her life. But eventually Jenny wondered, *How many shopping sprees does it take for a good life? How many doodads will bring me lasting joy? How many bobbles will I need to buy before I'm truly "bobbled out"?* After all, the thrill of buying and owning things wore off right away. And sometimes Jenny worried that her "storing up of treasures"' was becoming more than a hobby—it was an addiction and an idol.

Does that mean we as Christians need to adopt a legalistic view that says, "No pretty bobbles for you, girly"? No, it means we should follow the lead of the Holy Spirit, who has our best interests at heart—always.

Lord, sometimes I buy waaay more than I need. Forgive me. May Your Holy Spirit show me how to find balance in my life— when to shop, when to work, when to rest, and when to praise You for all Your good gifts! Amen.—AH

MOMENTS OF GRACE

From his fullness we have all received,
grace upon grace.
JOHN 1:16 NRSV

The older minister looked out over his congregation and smiled. He loved the folks in his church very much, and he always looked forward to the Sunday morning sermon. He truly loved to encourage and inspire his parishioners. In fact, it was one of the greatest joys of his life. But somewhere deep down he sighed a bit. Perhaps his sermons had gotten a bit tiresome or stale or repetitive, since he noticed a prominent member in the second row nodding off into a deep sleep. Some part of the minster wanted to wake up the sleeping man with a shout of glory or a pound of his fist on the podium, but then the minster remembered that the man worked two jobs to make ends meet for his family. Perhaps the greater good was to provide the poor man with a moment of peace and a few minutes' rest. Yes, he would offer that grace. That thought made the minister smile even brighter. It made his sermon more poignant, and it made his heart as light as a feather.

What grace can we offer others this week?

Lord, show me the people who need an extra helping
of grace today, for I know You have graciously
given me grace upon grace. Amen.—AH

MEETING GOD

*For the word of God is living and active, sharper than
any two-edged sword, piercing to the division of soul
and of spirit, of joints and of marrow, and discerning
the thoughts and intentions of the heart.*

HEBREWS 4:12 ESV

The author sitting behind the table looked at the long line of customers in the bookstore. Yep, that crowd was there for her, waiting patiently for her to sign her book. Yippee! The author flipped her hair and gushed and gave her signature some added panache. And that smile–you could have landed a jet at midnight with the beam of light flooding from her face! And the author's fans were just as giddy to meet her. In fact, they were willing to wait for hours for her to sign her latest bestseller.

So. . .would we wait in line to meet God if He had a bestseller? Of course! We would elbow and push our way to the front of the line for that opportunity. Wait a minute. God *does* have a bestseller. And we can meet with Him anytime we like. Uh-oh.

Yeah, we humans are a funny lot. Good thing there's grace. We need lots of it. Maybe even right this very minute. . .

*Lord, I'm sorry I sometimes forget to spend time reading Your
Living Word and that I've neglected to spend time in Your holy
presence. Thank You for Your gracious mercy. Amen.–AH*

A HUNDRED DIFFERENT WAYS

*"You shall love the L*ORD *your God with all your heart and with all your soul and with all your might."*

DEUTERONOMY 6:5 ESV

Grace is such a beautiful gift given to us by God. When someone gives us a wonderful present, we naturally want to thank the giver. In the case of grace, the gift is from God. Don't we love Him dearly for such an unexpected and undeserved offering? There are so many ways to thank God for His gentle mercies, for His forgiveness through the death and resurrection of His Son, for His everlasting love and promise of eternal life.

Why not whisper your gratitude to God as you wake up in the early dawn? Why not shout your praises to Him when you reach the summit after a long hike? You could write the Lord a love letter or record all your loving thoughts about Him in a journal. Perhaps creating a garden dedicated to the Lord would be in order, or hosting a party celebrating God's grace. Maybe you could thank the Lord by telling others about your life journey, or you could set aside a special day for some quiet time, basking in God's life-changing presence. There are a hundred ways to say, "Thank You, God." What will yours be?

Lord, I love You, and I thank You for all You've done for me! Amen.—AH

SPIRITUAL WARFARE

For we do not wrestle against flesh and blood, but against the rulers, against the authorities, against the cosmic powers over this present darkness, against the spiritual forces of evil in the heavenly places. Therefore take up the whole armor of God, that you may be able to withstand in the evil day, and having done all, to stand firm.
EPHESIANS 6:12–13 ESV

If we believe the Bible, we must believe there is indeed a supernatural world out there—an unseen world that is as real as the world in which we exist. And this invisible realm isn't empty. It's full of spiritual activity, as we read in Ephesians. Yes, there are angels, but there are also other entities that are not benevolent. As Christians, we must realize that the enemy—Satan—and his evil emissaries do not want us to be redeemed, to walk with God, or to tell others about His love and forgiveness. Sound fearsome? What can mere humans do?

To know more about how we can engage in spiritual warfare using God's holy armor, read Ephesians 6:12-18. Taking up this armor is not only a *great* way to live; it's the only way!

Lord, help me not to live in fear of spiritual warfare but to faithfully put on Your holy armor! Amen.—AH

WHAT HAVE I BECOME?

*But if we confess our sins to him, he can be depended
on to forgive us and to cleanse us from every wrong.
And it is perfectly proper for God to do this for us
because Christ died to wash away our sins.*

1 JOHN 1:9 TLB

The woman was a royal miser. She would even try to pick up a penny on a busy street with horns blaring at her. Mercy! Over time, the result of her penny-pinching efforts—after accumulating in a canning jar—came to a whopping three dollars and twenty-one cents. Which she didn't spend or give away, even when she wanted to treat a friend to a cup of coffee. But the woman wasn't just a cheapskate when it came to money; she was stingy with good deeds, kind words, love, and even forgiveness.

But one evening—for the first time in her life—she watched the holiday film *A Christmas Carol*. Watching Scrooge was a bit unnerving for her. She thought, *That character is behaving wretchedly!* An odd thing, though—Scrooge reminded her of someone. Uh-oh. As more and more of the film unfolded, conviction pinched her soul and repentance came calling. "Oh Lord, what have I become?" she cried. "Help me!"

There are times we all could cry out, "Oh Lord, what have I become? Help me!"

Lord, please help me to have a generous spirit. Amen.—AH

SOUL MIGRATION

Be wise when you engage with those outside
the faith community; make the most of every moment
and every encounter. When you speak the word,
speak it gracefully (as if seasoned with salt), so you
will know how to respond to everyone rightly.
COLOSSIANS 4:5-6 VOICE

Watching nature shows and seeing the great migrations of different animals can be a thrill. They travel closely together, knowing in some deep instinctual way just where they belong.

In the fall of mankind in Eden, we chose to separate ourselves from God, but somewhere deep down in our souls, we still know Who we belong to. And through the person of Jesus Christ and the power He gives us through His Holy Spirit, we can help with this soul migration back to God.

As believers we should be the most winsome of all creatures—full of laughter and joy. We should be the best at "seeing" folks and listening with our whole hearts. And love? People will know something is splendidly right with us when they come close. Our love will radiate Christ in every way, even down to our smiles.

So *are* we helping the Lord with this great migration of the soul?

Lord Jesus, please help me to speak graciously
and respond to people rightly so that I can be a
winsome and wonderful witness for You! Amen.—AH

GOD'S PERFECT JUSTICE

Everyone who makes a practice of sinning also practices lawlessness; sin is lawlessness.
1 JOHN 3:4 ESV

When it comes to God's grace, there are two kinds of people—folks who are truly remorseful when they have sinned and others who are merely sorry they got caught in their transgressions! Yes, the Lord will indeed forgive all our iniquities if we are sincerely repentant, but we will still face the consequences of our sins and a loving correction from the Lord. We might need to make an apology or offer some recompense. In some cases, we might even need to serve time in a correctional facility.

In the end, we can rejoice that justice goes hand in hand with grace. Otherwise our world would be full of confusion and fear and eventually anarchy. We can rejoice that in God's perfect justice lie mercy and grace. In the Lord's divine discipline reside help and healing. It is reassuring to know too that God—being the good parent He is—disciplines His children because He loves them dearly!

Lord, I am truly sorrowful for my sins, and I humbly ask You for forgiveness. If I need to submit to Your correction, please let me see it as loving and helpful and ultimately healing. In Jesus' holy name I pray. Amen.—AH

INTO THE ARMS OF GOD

*I led them with cords of human kindness, with ties
of love. To them I was like one who lifts a little child
to the cheek, and I bent down to feed them.*

HOSEA 11:4 NIV

Anne loved being with her baby. She loved listening to her coo, feeding her, whispering sweet nothings to her, kissing her soft cheek, watching her grow week by week, and simply being with her. Truth be told, Anne was happily lost in love. When Anne's child grew up and went off to college, she always found reasons to call her, but really sometimes it was just to hear her daughter's voice. Anne longed to help her daughter too, so when she was upset about anything, Anne made time to listen or guide or just quiet her gently with her love.

Since the very beginning of creation, God has wanted to have a sweet relationship with us. He has loved us and has wanted to be loved by us. To share our days and be ever near us.

How beautiful is God's love? How irresistible is the mercy of Christ?

*My dearest Lord Jesus, thank You for
Your love and the tender way in which You
watch over me. I love You too! Amen.—AH*

PERFUME POURED OUT

One of the Pharisees asked Jesus to come to his home for lunch and Jesus accepted the invitation. As they sat down to eat, a woman of the streets–a prostitute–heard he was there and brought an exquisite flask filled with expensive perfume. Going in, she knelt behind him at his feet, weeping, with her tears falling down upon his feet; and she wiped them off with her hair and kissed them and poured the perfume on them.

LUKE 7:36–38 TLB

In regard to our salvation, there is nothing we can do–no noble deeds or lofty thoughts or special words–to add to or improve upon what was accomplished through Christ's death and resurrection. But what we *can* do is come before the Lord with a humble attitude, a repentant heart, and thanksgiving for His mercy and grace.

And so it went with the humble and repentant and grateful woman depicted in Luke 7, who poured out her perfume and her tears on Christ's feet. Oh, may our very lives be a daily pouring out of gratitude–like costly perfume–for this gift of forgiveness that only Christ can offer.

Lord Jesus, I cannot thank You enough for Your redemption, which cost You Your very life. I love You with all my heart, and I look forward to spending an eternity with You in heaven! Amen.–AH

THE BEST PLACE TO BE

"The eternal God is your refuge,
and underneath are the everlasting arms."
DEUTERONOMY 33:27 NIV

The little boy was so tired and cranky and miserable, he decided that the best and most "wonderfulest" place to be was either on his daddy's lap or in his mom's arms. The boy's mom was close by on the couch, so he climbed up and snuggled close. He whimpered and fussed. Then he admitted to some sadness over letting the dog dig up some of her petunias, which she forgave him for straightaway. The mom held the boy near her heart, whispered her love, and encouraged him to sleep. Finally, he laid the last of his little-boy burdens down, cuddled nearer to his mom, and closed his eyes.

This tiny story makes our hearts sigh. Why? Because we hope that God feels the same love for us. Actually, He does—even more. God is always there waiting for us to lay down our burdens and come to Him for everything. Can you sense His mighty arms around you and hear His whispers of love? Yes, being in the arms of God is the best and most "wonderfulest" place to be!

Oh Lord, I am so tried and world-weary. I am so
glad to rest in Your everlasting arms. Amen.–AH

BE STILL AND KNOW

*"Be still, and know that I am God. I will be exalted
among the nations, I will be exalted in the earth!"*

PSALM 46:10 ESV

"Deep breath. Deep breath." Allison whispered the words to herself as she came awake from a horrible dream. She rolled over in the bed and the scenes replayed themselves in her imagination. She knew the dream by heart, of course. She'd had it so many times before. In it, she was thrust back to her past, to a time she'd sooner forget, to a relationship she'd sooner forget.

Once fully awake, Allison took a shower and did her best to wash away the memories of yesterday. It took some time in prayer before she finally felt peace again.

Maybe you can relate to Allison's plight. You have things in your past you'd sooner forget too—things God has already forgiven you for. The enemy tries to replay them, like rolls of film, but you refuse to go there. You're a child of the Almighty, forgiven and set free. When the enemy of your soul tries to torment you, speak the truth: "I'm set free, in Jesus' name!" Even demons have to flee at that mighty name!

*Lord, I'm so grateful the past is in the past.
Teach me how to walk in freedom, I pray. Amen.—JT*

THE MEDIATOR MADE THE WAY

*For there is one God and one Mediator
between God and men, the Man Christ Jesus,*
1 TIMOTHY 2:5 NKJV

Laurie arrived in the courtroom, terrified to face the judge after what she'd done. Her guilt made the process even more unnerving. No doubt he would give her the punishment she deserved. She'd made the wrong choice, given in to the temptation to do something both immoral and illegal.

What comfort the attorney at her side brought. He patted her hand, whispered, "Let me speak on your behalf," then approached the bench for her. A short while later, she received her sentence. She would have to pay a price for her crime, but nothing as bad as she had feared. Having a mediator had made the whole experience less painful.

Does Laurie's story remind you of your walk with Christ? You came to Him guilty—convicted of your sin. He approached the bench on your behalf and took on the role of mediator. He actually paid the price for your sin and you were set free—forgiven, once and for all. What an amazing price He paid on your behalf. How blessed you are!

*Lord, how can I ever thank You for serving as my attorney?
You mediated on my behalf and spared me from an
eternity apart from You. Thank You! Amen.—JT*

THE NEW HAS COME

Therefore, if anyone is in Christ, he is a new creation.
The old has passed away; behold, the new has come.
2 CORINTHIANS 5:17 ESV

Gillian had a hard time thinking of herself as "new." When she glanced in the mirror, all she saw were the haunting memories of yesterday—the woman she used to be. It took some time to realize God had truly wiped away those sins and transformed her into a whole new person.

Perhaps you feel a bit like Gillian. The reflection in the mirror shows little but regrets. It's time to be set free. God didn't forgive you to leave you stuck in the miry clay. He doesn't want you to be bogged down with your yesterdays. It's time to look forward to a hopeful tomorrow.

Perhaps you're wondering how to go about that. You have to start by admitting you can't do life on your own. You were never meant to. Call on the Lord. He's close by, ready to help. He has also given you the gift of His Holy Spirit, who longs to bring comfort and to offer direction. You are not alone. With His help, you can walk in newness.

Thank You for the gift of Your Spirit, Lord!
I know brighter days are ahead. Amen.—JT

PRESSING TOWARD THE PRIZE

*No, dear brothers and sisters, I have not achieved it, but I
focus on this one thing: Forgetting the past and looking
forward to what lies ahead, I press on to reach the end of
the race and receive the heavenly prize for which God,
through Christ Jesus, is calling us.*

PHILIPPIANS 3:13–14 NLT

If anyone understood the depth of guilt and shame, King David did.
Though known as "a man after God's own heart," this on-again, off-again
king also knew the agony of giving in to temptation. After he happened
to see Bathsheba bathing, he lusted after her beauty and decided to
take her as his own.

Bathsheba conceived, and David ultimately used his authority as
king to have her husband, Uriah, sent to the front lines of battle, knowing
the poor man would not survive. As he hoped, Uriah died, Bathsheba
was free to marry David, and they had a child together. No doubt David
was relieved his plan worked.

Jump ahead. Bathsheba delivered a male child. When that child
died a short while later, David was reminded of his sin against Uriah.
He had to face the inevitable. . .his own guilt. King David fully repented
before the Lord and was restored, but he never again saw that baby boy.

Here's good news: David's life on the other side of forgiveness
was filled with excitement and adventure. God can use even the most
wicked if they truly turn from their sin and choose fullness of life in Him.

*Lord, I'm so glad there's life on the other side of sin.
That gives me such hope. Amen.—JT*

FORGIVEN TO BRING HONOR

*Now to the King eternal, immortal, invisible, the only
God, be honor and glory for ever and ever. Amen.*
1 TIMOTHY 1:17 NIV

During her college years, Bridget slipped into a dangerous lifestyle. She gave in to the temptation to be like her roommates. They loved to party, often with no thought to safety or common sense. One night on the way home from a particularly rowdy night of drinking, she opted to drive. Bridget caused an accident that nearly ended her life. Thank goodness, no one else was badly hurt, but this horrific incident served to wake her up from her slumber.

Bridget spent the next several years reliving the accident, time after time. When she closed her eyes, she replayed it over and over again. She couldn't seem to break free from that moment of impact. It haunted her.

Perhaps you've had an experience like Bridget's. Maybe you're having a hard time letting go of the pain caused by your own actions. Jesus wants to set you free today—not just from the haunting memories, but from the pain of a poor decision. Meet with Him. Get real with Him. Pour out your heart and watch as He picks up the pieces of your pain and redirects your thoughts. There really is hope on the other side of poor decisions if you ask for, and accept, God's forgiveness.

*Thank You for setting me free from my
poor decisions, Lord! Amen.—JT*

FREEDOM FROM SHAME

*Instead of shame and dishonor, you will enjoy a double share
of honor. You will possess a double portion of prosperity
in your land, and everlasting joy will be yours.*
ISAIAH 61:7 NLT

She walked to the well at the usual time—late in the afternoon, when none of the other women were out and about. Avoiding the stares and gossip of the locals had become something of a challenge, but she had it down to a science. When she arrived, a stranger greeted her—a male, no less. "Draw from the well," He said. "Give me a drink."

Was she hearing correctly? This man, a Jew, wanted her—a Samaritan—to offer Him a drink of water? As she served Him, the stranger began to share things about her life that He couldn't possibly have known. "You have had five husbands, and the man you are living with now is not your husband."

Shame enveloped her. Guilt locked her in a tight embrace. How did He know? Then the man—whose eyes were filled with love and grace—continued to engage her in conversation, His words laced with forgiveness.

Maybe you've had an encounter like that with the Lord. He's read your mail. He's called you on the carpet. And then, out of His deep grace, He's offered forgiveness. What a gracious God we serve!

*I'm so happy you've set me free from shame,
Father! How I praise You! Amen.—JT*

SALVATION'S JOY

Restore to me the joy of your salvation,
and uphold me with a willing spirit.
PSALM 51:12 ESV

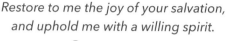

Have you ever watched murky dishwater gurgle its way down the drain? What started as fluffy, lightweight bubbles are now greasy, stinky blobs, struggling to make their way down, down, down into the abyss, never to be seen again. It's a transformation from pure and lovely to dirty and spoiled.

That's what happens when you allow guilt and condemnation to replace the joy you once felt as a new believer. The drain gets clogged. Many of the happy, positive things you enjoy in life come to an abrupt halt. Your usual bubbly joy is replaced with something dark and murky, and it's hard to push it through the drain.

Today God wants to restore your joy. In fact, He longs to take away the stain of sin altogether and replace it with forgiveness. You can feel new again. You can bubble with excitement once more. Allow God to do a deep work—let Him take the pain of yesterday and wash it away into the abyss—then watch as He restores the joy of your salvation.

I'm so grateful for Your restorative power, Lord.
You're bringing new life and new joy.
How I praise You! Amen.—JT

FORGIVEN TO GROW

*Rather, you must grow in the grace and knowledge
of our Lord and Savior Jesus Christ. All glory
to him, both now and forever! Amen.*

2 PETER 3:18 NLT

Have you ever considered the fact that you were forgiven for a purpose? God didn't just wipe your slate clean so that you could spend eternity in heaven with Him. He has great things for you to do—right here, right now.

One of the primarily goals of the forgiven should be spiritual growth. What would be the point of a fresh start if you were only going to lie there and soak in the kindness of God without offering something in return? In many ways you are like a tiny plant poking its way out of the soil, face turned toward the sunlight. The possibilities are endless when you're planted in good soil and drinking in proper nutrients. You can develop, grow, learn new things—then share them with a world in need.

How do you begin the growth process? Get in God's Word. Discover His plans for your life. Take steps of faith toward Christ-centered goals. Don't give up when the going gets tough. Keep on keeping on.

God forgave you so that you could do glorious things for Him. Turn that face toward the sun. It's time to grow, sister!

*Thank You for the reminder that You want
me to grow, Lord. I won't give up. I'll plant my
roots deep in You and grow, grow, grow. Amen.—JT*

MY SOUL WAITS

I wait for the LORD, my whole being waits, and in his word I put
my hope. I wait for the Lord more than watchmen wait for the
morning, more than watchmen wait for the morning.
PSALM 130:5–6 NIV

Kendra was sure she'd heard from God. She prayed, sought His input, but couldn't seem to get a clear sense of direction. She eventually forged ahead, convinced God would see the good in it. Only when she was shoulder-deep in the negative consequences of her decision did Kendra realize she'd made a catastrophic mistake. She'd jumped ahead of God and stepped into something she should have avoided altogether. Oh, if only she had waited!

One of the ways we get ourselves into trouble is by getting ahead of God. We don't wait on His guidance, His leading. Instead, we forge ahead on our own, convinced we've heard from Him when, in fact, we haven't. We get impatient. We plow forward when we should be still in His presence.

How do you know if you've heard from the Lord? You'll feel complete peace, along with a prompting to step forward. This doesn't mean you'll always get it right. But when you do get ahead of Him, He's right there, ready to forgive and offer grace.

Lord, I want to move at Your prompting and in Your
timing. Tune my ear to Your voice, I pray. Amen.–JT

THE CONVICTION OF
THINGS NOT SEEN

*Now faith is the assurance of things hoped for,
the conviction of things not seen. For by it the people of
old received their commendation. By faith we understand
that the universe was created by the word of God, so that
what is seen was not made out of things that are visible.*
HEBREWS 11:1–3 ESV

Wouldn't it be wonderful if, at the moment of forgiveness, God wrote on the wall: "In case you ever doubt it, I have completely forgiven you!" Then, in moments of doubt, you would have something tangible to look at, a sign to bring assurance that forgiveness really had been granted, once and for all.

The problem is, forgiveness can't be seen with the human eye. There are no super-duper x-ray glasses to help you make out the words, "Child, you are forgiven." You can only "see" them imprinted on your heart.

So how can you begin the process of believing? How can you set your spiritual eyes to see? Start in God's Word. Dive deep and find the scriptures about His amazing forgiving power. Read them. Post them on your bathroom mirror, on your refrigerator, at your workplace. Memorize them so that you never forget—you are truly forgiven, now and forevermore.

*I can't see it, Lord, but I know You've forgiven
me because Your Word confirms it. I'm so
grateful for Your forgiveness. Amen.—JT*

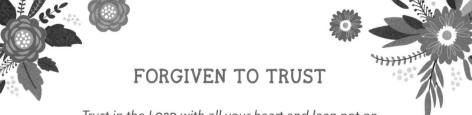

FORGIVEN TO TRUST

*Trust in the LORD with all your heart and lean not on
your own understanding; in all your ways submit
to him, and he will make your paths straight.*
PROVERBS 3:5–6 NIV

She'd waited years for a child, putting up with ridicule and torment from other women. Hannah wondered if she would ever see her dreams come true. Would she know the joy of motherhood?

In desperation, she went to the temple. There she poured out her heart to the Lord with such angst and emotion that some thought she had been drinking. Even the priest, Eli, accused her of being drunk. It didn't take long to convince him she was simply in anguish. Eli prayed for her, and Hannah eventually conceived a son, Samuel, who went on to do great things for God.

Hannah is a great example of trusting God, even in the hardest circumstances. Perhaps you can relate. No doubt you've been through seasons when hope seemed lost. But God didn't forgive you and offer you new life to leave you hopeless. Lift those eyes! Trust Him with all your heart and the Lord will move on your behalf, just as He did for Hannah. God may not answer your prayer exactly as you want Him to or within your specific timing, but He will be faithful!

*Lord, I choose to trust. You didn't bring
me this far to leave me. Amen.–JT*

THINK ON THESE THINGS

Finally, brothers and sisters, whatever is true, whatever is noble, whatever is right, whatever is pure, whatever is lovely, whatever is admirable—if anything is excellent or praiseworthy—think about such things.

PHILIPPIANS 4:8 NIV

Where your thoughts go, your actions will follow. Lisa found this out the hard way. Happily married to the man of her dreams, she should have been blissfully happy. They had a wonderful home, three great kids, and precious friends.

In spite of all these things, her thoughts kept drifting back to a former relationship and a decision she'd made to give her virginity away to the wrong person. Though she had asked for God's forgiveness, though she'd shared the story with her husband before they married, she couldn't let go of the fact that she'd given away pieces of her heart—and her body—to someone she wasn't married to.

It took some time before Lisa finally managed to let go of the pain of the past. With a great deal of prayer and a lot of time in God's Word, she finally shifted her thoughts away from the past and toward the present.

God can do the same for you. Ask Him to shift your thinking to the things that matter, and your actions will follow.

Thank You for the reminder that my thinking can change, Lord! Amen.—JT

BEYOND PRISON WALLS

"But forget all that—it is nothing compared to what I am going to do. For I am about to do something new. See, I have already begun! Do you not see it? I will make a pathway through the wilderness. I will create rivers in the dry wasteland."

ISAIAH 43:18-19 NLT

No doubt he heard the singing. Surely he felt the earthquake and saw the prison doors flying open. But the jailer—the very one who had locked Paul and Silas in their cell—knew his life would be over if prisoners escaped on his watch. In desperation, he prepared to take his own life. Only when Paul called out, "Do not harm yourself, for we are all here" (Acts 16:28 ESV), did he realize his story might have a tolerable ending.

Instead of ending his life, the jailer found new life that night. . .through Jesus Christ. He discovered true freedom by watching how his Christian prisoners responded to their situation.

There is life beyond prison walls. No matter what road you've walked, no matter who you've hurt or who's hurt you, better days are ahead. No matter which side of the prison walls you find yourself on today, understand that God sees you and longs for you to be forgiven and free.

Father, I thank You for setting prisoners free.
Use me, as You used Paul and Silas, to make a
difference in someone's life, I pray. Amen.—JT

FORGIVEN TO FIND PEACE

Casting all your anxieties on him,
because he cares for you.
1 PETER 5:7 ESV

She replayed the conversation over and over in her head. It had been two years since her mother's death, but Marilyn couldn't forgive herself for the harsh words she had spoken years prior. Mom couldn't help it that she had Alzheimer's. She didn't mean to cause extra grief or work. Why then had Marilyn spoken so harshly to her own mother when the situation was beyond anyone's control? Oh, if only she could take back some of the careless words she'd spoken. But there was no taking them back now. Mom was gone, after all.

Maybe you can relate. Perhaps you have played the role of caregiver and you know the anguish of a harsh word or lack of patience. It's hard to imagine God would forgive that, but He will. . .if you ask. Those painful things you've spoken to a loved one? Even if they are no longer here to receive your apology, let God know that you want to be forgiven. He will wash away every stain and make you new again. And no doubt He will give you plenty of opportunities to speak to loved ones in a kinder way moving forward.

Father, I'm so ashamed of the harsh words I've spoken
to loved ones. Please forgive me, I pray. Amen.—JT

CONTINUAL HOPE

But I will hope continually, and will
praise You yet more and more.
PSALM 71:14 NKJV

Have you ever pondered the notion that hope is meant to be ever increasing? It's supposed to grow and grow and grow as our faith deepens. Why isn't that always the case? After all, we're more often inclined to lose hope when things don't go our way. We give up when the odds seem to be against us. But God longs for us to place our hope in Him to the point where we grow daily in our trust, no matter what circumstances we're facing or how difficult the task before us.

Tough situation? Have hope. Struggling to forgive (others or yourself)? Have hope. Wondering where the next mortgage payment will come from? Let your hope grow as you wait on the Lord.

No matter your background, no matter how hopeless things have seemed in the past, today can be different. Your hope can increase. Your joy can overflow. Forgiveness will set you free to dream as you've never dreamed before and to dip into the well of hope once again.

Lord, I've needed a rejuvenation of hope. I want my hope
to grow and my praises to increase as I age, not just when
circumstances dictate, but at all times, Father. Amen.—JT

FORGIVEN TO SHARE
THE GOOD NEWS

"But you will receive power when the Holy Spirit comes on you; and you will be my witnesses in Jerusalem, and in all Judea and Samaria, and to the ends of the earth."
ACTS 1:8 NIV

The great revivalist preacher Jonathan Edwards was a key player in what has become known as the First Great Awakening. His journey began when revival broke out in 1731. A witness to this spectacular move of God, Edwards began to study the process of conversion. He recorded his observations and learned from them, then spread the gospel with fervor, longing for all to come to know Christ. Edwards's sermon "Sinners in the Hands of an Angry God" is a classic example of the passion that fueled him to reach others.

No one can fully understand revival until they have experienced forgiveness from Almighty God. Once forgiven, we are free to proclaim the mighty work the Lord has done in our hearts and minds. This was the message Edwards preached.

Where are you in the journey? Has God set you free from the past? Has He done a mighty work in your heart? If so, rejoice! God has set you free so that you can share the good news of what He has done. Don't stay silent. Let others know. God is so good! Spread the word!

I won't keep the news to myself, Lord. Thank You for giving me freedom so that I can reach others. Amen.–JT

FORGIVEN TO BELIEVE

*And it is impossible to please God without faith.
Anyone who wants to come to him must believe that God
exists and that he rewards those who sincerely seek him.*
HEBREWS 11:6 NLT

Little children are willing to believe just about anything they're told. From Santa to the tooth fairy, their innocent little hearts accept it all. When Mommy says, "I love you!" they never question it. When Daddy says, "I'm going to take you fishing next Saturday," they believe it. Every word spoken over them is gospel truth.

Oftentimes we forget to come to God as a child would approach a loving parent. We let unforgiveness (toward ourselves or others) cloud our ability to think with such simple purity.

The Lord wants you to have the faith of an innocent child. He wants "believing" to be as simple as a toddler believing his mother will feed him his favorite lunch. What's holding you back today? Maybe it's time to look up at Daddy God and take Him at His word.

*Father, I come to You as a child, my heart
completely full of love and trust. I will
take You at Your word, Lord. Amen.—JT*

WITH ALL YOUR HEART

Trust in the LORD with all your heart,
and do not lean on your own understanding.
PROVERBS 3:5 ESV

Norah spent hours a day thinking. . .and thinking. . .and rethinking. After a rough conversation with her grown daughter, she replayed their words in her mind many times over. What could she have said–or done–differently? After a meeting with her boss, she couldn't seem to shake a couple of his negative comments. They plagued her. Was he unhappy with her performance in the workplace? She wondered if she might lose her job. Her worries lasted late into the night and caused her to go without sleep.

It wasn't enough for Norah to think about things. She made it her goal to solve every puzzle and to fix every problem. Only, she couldn't seem to accomplish much with her thoughts riveted on the problems. Instead, the missed sleep made her feel even worse the next day.

Maybe you can relate to Norah. God has freed you from the sins and pain of the past. Your yesterdays are behind you. But old habits die hard. Your desire to fix things–to hyper-focus on them–needs to go. Today God can give you a fresh start. Come to Him. Offer Him your thought-life. Say, "Lord, I choose to lean on Your understanding, not my own." Then watch as He transforms your thinking.

Thank You for changing my
stinking thinking, Lord! Amen.–JT

FORGIVEN TO BE SET FREE

*There is therefore now no condemnation
for those who are in Christ Jesus.*
ROMANS 8:1 ESV

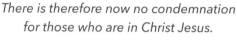

Susan spent her whole life trying to perform. Nothing she did was good enough for her mother. Over time, Susan's disappointment in herself nearly crippled her. No matter how hard she worked, she felt as if she'd fallen short. Despite her many accomplishments, she still beat herself up. This was especially true in her spiritual life. She couldn't seem to accept the notion that the work of Jesus on the cross was enough to forgive her for her sins. Instead, she depended on her own good works to save her.

Perhaps you can relate to Susan. You want to believe that you don't have to work to earn God's favor, but it's so hard. Is it really possible to relinquish your heart to Him and receive forgiveness. . .just like that?

God never intended for you to slave away to earn His favor. His work on the cross was more than enough to save you. Don't get hung up on what you need to do. Just reach out and accept His free gift of salvation, then watch as His work is established in you.

*Lord, You want me to be set free. There's no
condemnation in You. I'm so grateful I don't
have to earn Your love, Father. Amen.—JT*

UNWAVERING

But let him ask in faith, with no doubting,
for he who doubts is like a wave of the
sea driven and tossed by the wind.
JAMES 1:6 NKJV

Perhaps you've been there—tossed about by the wind, up one day, down the next. One day walking in victory, the next in defeat. The up-and-down motion can be exhausting.

God doesn't want you to bounce around like a child on a teeter-totter. His ultimate goal is for stability in your life. It comes by latching onto the promises you find in scripture. They will hold your feet steady.

If you're doubting where you stand with God today, if you're struggling with the "Has He really forgiven me?" question, then rest easy. If you've asked, it's already done. God doesn't go back on His word.

If you haven't yet asked for forgiveness for the sins of yesterday, there's no better time than the present. Come to Him—just as today's scripture says—in faith. Don't doubt. Come with the assurance that He adores you and wants you to experience new life in Him. When you leave your yesterdays in His hands, you will become as steady as a rock—unwavering, unmovable. What a terrific way to live!

Thank You for steadying me, Lord. I choose to trust in You.
I won't doubt. I'll take You at Your word, Father. Amen.—JT

A LOVE LETTER

I am writing to you, dear children, because your
sins have been forgiven on account of his name.
1 JOHN 2:12 NIV

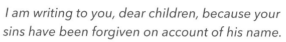

Have you ever taken the time to write a letter. . .just because? Maybe you wanted to bless that special child or grandchild so you sent an unexpected card in the mail, one guaranteed to make them smile. Perhaps you watched a friend go through a particularly tough season and you wanted to offer encouragement, so you sent a handwritten letter, letting her know how much you care.

These little notes of encouragement mean everything to the recipient, especially when they arrive in God's perfect timing. Talk about a game-changer!

Did you realize that the Author of the universe, the Creator of all, took the time to send you a love letter? It's true! His Word is filled with assurances of his adoration and undying affection for you, His child. It's a reminder of His amazing love and His forgiveness for your sins.

No matter what you've done, no matter what road you've walked, you can always turn to His Word for the comfort and encouragement you need to get through the day.

I'm so grateful for Your love letter, Lord. I keep it close to my
heart and read the words over and over again. Thank You
for caring enough to send Your Word, Lord. Amen.–JT

COME INTO AGREEMENT

"Agree with God, and be at peace;
thereby good will come to you."
JOB 22:21 ESV

There's great power in confession. Getting things off your chest, speaking your confessions aloud, can change the course of your life.

When you've been forgiven, you should shout it from the rooftops, not hold it inside. When you say with your mouth, "God has forgiven me!" you're not just sharing the news with others; you're reconfirming the message to your own heart. It's a confidence booster and a great reminder that the past is exactly where it belongs, in the past.

The Bible assures us that we will be saved by the word of our testimony. If we don't share what God has done, then people won't hear the Good News of Jesus Christ.

Come into agreement with God today. Begin to speak forgiveness—over yourself and those around you. There is great power in speaking His truth.

Lord, I want to be a witness for You. I come into
agreement with You. I'm ready to share what
You've done in my life. Amen.—JT

FORGIVEN TO BELONG

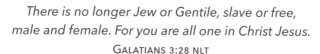

There is no longer Jew or Gentile, slave or free,
male and female. For you are all one in Christ Jesus.
GALATIANS 3:28 NLT

Take a peek at the story of Rahab (in the second chapter of Joshua). Working as a prostitute in the city of Jericho, she wasn't a likely candidate to be included in the lineage of the Savior. But God used Rahab in spite of her past, in spite of her sins. She befriended the Israelite spies (enemies of her own people) and hid them in her home. The spies were saved and went on to take over the city, all because of one woman's bravery—a woman who would have been written off by most.

God doesn't discriminate. He forgives your sins and casts them as far as the east is from the west. And with that forgiveness comes an unexpected blessing—inclusion. When you're forgiven, when you're swept into the family of God, you're given family rights. You're a sister, a daughter, a friend.

Today, take the time to thank God for including you. You were forgiven to belong. Take full advantage of your "belonging" by connecting with fellow believers as often as you can.

Thank You, Father, for sweeping me into the family.
I'm so glad I belong. Amen.—JT

FIRM IN THE FAITH

Be watchful, stand firm in the faith,
act like men, be strong.
1 CORINTHIANS 16:13 ESV

Picture a guard stationed on the city wall. He has one job, to watch out for intruders. His eyes are wide open. He's not letting anyone through unless they're on the approved list. Now imagine your heart has a guard—the Holy Spirit. But you've nudged Him aside and have allowed a few things to slip through—bitterness, jealousy, unforgiveness, and a host of other tormenters besides. You didn't mean to let your guard down, but the enemy tiptoed in and took control while you were looking the other way.

God longs for His kiddos to stand firm in the faith. The strength you have in Him comes from the inner knowledge that He loved you enough to die for you, enough to give you new life on the other side of your pain. Your freedom is worth guarding. It's worth protecting.

Be firm. Don't relent. Don't give in. You were offered a second chance so that you could live—truly, fully, unreservedly. Eyes wide open, sister! Don't let the enemy slip in unnoticed!

Father, thank You! Stand as a watchman over my heart today,
I pray. Guard me. Keep me from the enemy's snares.
I will stand firm with Your help. Amen.—JT

MY HOPE IS IN YOU

"And now, Lord, what do I wait for? My hope is in You."
PSALM 39:7 NKJV

We place our hope in so many things—other people, our work, even our own talents and abilities. When we're children, we place our hope in our parents, for they are the ones to guard, protect, and provide. As we get older, we begin to place our hope in other people, including members of the opposite sex. When/if we marry, many of our hopes are projected onto our spouse. Even after we have children our hope is often misplaced. We wish for things we don't already have—a bigger home, a nicer car, and so on.

There's nothing wrong with wishing and hoping. Just remember to keep your hope rooted in the One who gives only good gifts—like forgiveness, peace, and joy. He didn't save you to leave you hanging. He has good things in store for you. But don't allow those good things to take precedence over your relationship with Him.

Keep on hoping. Keep on believing. . .in Him. When you put Him first (in His rightful place as Lord, Savior, and forgiver of sins), everything you need will be given to you.

Lord, I'm grateful for the reminder that I should be seeking You,
not the things You can offer. I put my hope in You, Lord.
Guard the desires of my heart, I pray. Amen.—JT

HE REJOICES OVER YOU

*"The Lord your God is with you, the Mighty Warrior who saves.
He will take great delight in you; in his love he will no longer
rebuke you, but will rejoice over you with singing."*

ZEPHANIAH 3:17 NIV

Cora wasn't sure she would ever be able to have children. Years passed without a baby joining the family. When she and her husband finally adopted little Robbie, her heart was full to the brim. As he reached the toddler stage, she would sweep him into her arms and dance around the living room, completely overjoyed to be with him. In those moments all of his naughty toddler-antics were forgotten. All that remained was the celebration of her love for him.

That's how it is with Daddy God. He rejoices over you with singing and celebration. Instead of focusing on your disappointments or failures, He chooses to throw a party in your honor. What would be the point of sweeping you into the family if not to love you with full-out abandon?

The next time you picture God as a stern taskmaster, brush that image aside and focus on Him as your loving Daddy, forgiver of wrongs. Picture Him singing and dancing over you, then sweeping you into His arms. That's the kind of God you serve!

*Father, I love the image of You dancing and singing over me.
Thank You for loving me, Your child. Amen.—JT*

WEIGHTLESS LIVING

*Therefore, since we are surrounded by so great a cloud
of witnesses, let us also lay aside every weight, and sin
which clings so closely, and let us run with endurance
the race that is set before us, looking to Jesus.*
HEBREWS 12:1–2 ESV

Andrea stared at the crumbs on the plate in front of her. "Ugh. I did it again, Lord. I told myself I wasn't going to eat that slice of pie, but I just couldn't seem to resist." Why did she keep giving in to the same old temptation? As always, she struggled to forgive herself and wondered if God could forgive her as well.

Maybe you've walked a mile in Andrea's shoes. You've committed to a plan to lose weight and get healthy. Then—bam—a moment of weakness.

God does want His girls to be healthy, but He's not the taskmaster we make Him out to be. He's not logging your calories and carbs. That's not to say you should give up, but don't beat yourself up. God isn't sitting in heaven with a stick in His hand, ready to poke you whenever you eat a cookie. And remember, tomorrow's a brand-new day, filled with possibilities. Just begin again. And in the meantime, receive the forgiveness He offers. It's calorie free!

*Father, I'm so grateful You're not clocking my calories and carbs!
Help me to stick to a healthy eating plan and forgive me
when I slip back into old habits, I pray. Amen.–JT*

FORMER THINGS
ARE PASSED AWAY

*"He will wipe every tear from their eyes,
and there will be no more death or sorrow or
crying or pain. All these things are gone forever."*
REVELATION 21:4 NLT

Cherie walked out of the 12-step class, her heart in her throat. Confessing her latest slipup had been hard, but the class members offered nothing but encouragement and support. She knew they would be there for her regardless, and she wanted to do her best from now on.

If you've ever struggled with addiction—to alcohol, drugs, overeating, pornography, or any other vice—then you know Cherie's pain. Walking the straight and narrow isn't always easy, and slipups do happen. But God is gracious. He continues to extend His hand and offer new hope, new plans, new opportunities to do the right thing.

You can get through this. Whatever you're struggling with, you can overcome it with God's help. He will forgive. . .and forgive again. But don't use that as an excuse to keep sinning. Instead, turn your eyes to Him and allow Him to energize you with Spirit-filled power to overcome the temptation in front of you.

*Father, I'm an overcomer in Your name! My addictions
really can be a thing of the past. Thank You for your
forgiveness when I stumble and fall. Amen.—JT*

THAT I MAY GAIN HIM

What is more, I consider everything a loss because of the surpassing worth of knowing Christ Jesus my Lord, for whose sake I have lost all things. I consider them garbage, that I may gain Christ.
<small>PHILIPPIANS 3:8 NIV</small>

Maggie groaned as she checked the balance of her bank account. Why, oh why did she live so close to the edge? Why couldn't she get her impulsive shopping habits under control? She didn't need that latest pair of shoes. And she certainly could've done without those knickknacks for her coffee table. Her house was filled with enough trinkets and treasures already. She felt sick inside for causing the financial woes. Maggie wondered if God could keep on forgiving her if she kept overspending.

No doubt you've experienced the pain of Maggie's journey. You've given in to the temptation to purchase items you didn't really need. You've offered excuses as you've set that new trinket on the shelf. But you've secretly wondered why you can't get past the need to acquire more and more.

God can curb your shopping appetite if you ask Him to. He's right there, ready to offer sage advice when you need it. He's whispering, "Do you really need those new shoes? Didn't you just buy a new pair last month?" Or He's saying, "Why not skip the meal out and cook dinner at home?"

There will be shopping slipups, but God wants to deliver you from poor habits, if you will let Him. Will you let Him?

Lord, thank You for forgiving me when I overspend or make unwise decisions. Guide me, I pray. Amen.—JT

LIFE AND PEACE

For to set the mind on the flesh is death, but to
set the mind on the Spirit is life and peace.
ROMANS 8:6 ESV

Are you searching behind every nook and cranny for peace? Has it eluded you? There's only one place you'll find it—on the other side of forgiveness. Until you've experienced true freedom in Christ, peace will continue to elude you.

Don't believe it? Think back to your childhood. Remember that lie you told your mom? Remember how it plagued you for days until you finally confessed the truth? Remember how good it felt to finally get that icky thing off your chest? You experienced true life and peace on the other side of your mother's forgiveness, and the same is true of your relationship with Daddy God. He longs to forgive, and will keep on waiting, no matter how long it takes for you to come to Him.

Find peace today. Go to God with the thing that's weighing you down. Hold it up to Him and say, "Father, I've messed up. I need the peace that only You can bring. Forgive me, Lord." In that moment, He'll bathe you in supernatural, Spirit-filled peace like you've never known before.

What's holding you back? Run to Him today and experience a whole new way of living.

Father, I want (and need) Your peace. Today I offer my
sinful heart to You. I accept Your forgiveness and
receive Your supernatural peace! Amen.—JT

HOLY MEMORY LOSS

"I, even I, am He who blots out your transgressions
for My own sake; and I will not remember your sins."
Isaiah 43:25 NKJV

Have you ever been accused of being forgetful? Maybe you planned a lunch date with a friend but it slipped your mind at the last minute. Or perhaps you told your kiddos that you would take them to the park, only to forget.

Sometimes we get busy and overlook things. That's to be expected. But what if you had the capability of *truly* forgetting all the bad things you'd ever done? (Wouldn't that be lovely?)

God has supernatural memory loss. The Bible says He forgets our sins. He doesn't just forgive them; He forgets they ever happened in the first place. That's a miracle! When you think about forgiveness from the Lord's perspective, it's easy to see you're just wasting time when you fret over things He's already forgiven. Picture Him saying, "What? What's that? I'm not sure what you're talking about."

It's done. It's over. He has forgiven you and let it go. It's time you did too.

Father, thank You for the reminder that You have holy,
supernatural memory loss. Help me to forgive
myself and to forget as well. Amen.–JT

OUR GREAT HIGH PRIEST

Here is the main point: We have a High Priest
who sat down in the place of honor beside
the throne of the majestic God in heaven.
HEBREWS 8:1 NLT

Judy could have kicked herself. A financial error—a simple accounting mistake—threw off the balance in her checking account and caused a check to bounce. She didn't mean for it to happen, but the error caused additional fallout in her checking account that took weeks to remedy. With her life in such a crazy-busy state, she hardly had time to keep up with the important things. Her messy house was another indicator that things were out of alignment. And the laundry? Well, piles of it greeted her each day. She promised herself she'd get her act together. . .soon.

Maybe you're like Judy. You're overwhelmed by life. You spend day after day kicking yourself for not having it together. Things slip through the cracks and you wonder if you're the only one who can't get your act together. Your friends post lovely photos on social media of their beautiful, spotless homes, of their dream vacations, and you feel like such a loser.

It's time to lift your head, sister! Instead of focusing on all the things you're doing wrong, take a moment to celebrate the things you got right this week. God is not mad at you for the things that slip through the cracks. He'll give you the tools you need to get things done if you place them in His hands, and He'll (gladly!) forgive you if the laundry waits until morning.

Father, I'm so relieved You offer grace,
not judgment. Thank You, Lord. Amen.—JT

NEW LIFE, NEW ME

I have been crucified with Christ and I no longer live, but Christ lives in me. The life I now live in the body, I live by faith in the Son of God, who loved me and gave himself for me.
GALATIANS 2:20 NIV

The compelling storyline of the musical *Les Miserables* stands the test of time. At the start of the tale, Jean Valjean, a peasant, has just been released from jail. He was imprisoned for stealing bread to feed his family. Rejected by all, he ends up sleeping on the street until a priest takes him in. Jean makes a poor decision, to steal valuable silverware and candlesticks from the priest. Instead of turning him over to the police, the priest gives Jean a second chance while uttering these words: "Make an honest man of yourself."

Jean Valjean never forgets the words of the priest. They propel him to make something of his life. Likewise, God calls us to live lives worthy of our calling. He longs for fellowship with us, and that can happen only if we turn from our sin. Like Valjean, we can have a second chance, a new opportunity to get things right. How beautiful, the forgiveness of God that offers grace, time and time again.

Father, I want to live a life worthy of the forgiveness You've so graciously bestowed. Like Jean Valjean I long to make something of my life. Amen.—JT

FORGIVE. . .AS YOU
HAVE BEEN FORGIVEN

For I know the plans I have for you, declares the Lord, plans for
welfare and not for evil, to give you a future and a hope.
JEREMIAH 29:11 ESV

Winnie came from a broken family. Her father left when she was only three and her mom couldn't seem to get her act together. As a result, Winnie and her siblings eventually ended up in foster care. She never managed to shake the stigma that something was wrong with her, that she was destined to live as a loner in the world.

Only when Winnie came to Christ did she begin to understand the concept of inclusion. God swept her into a larger family and began to heal her wounds. He helped her forgive her parents for the many things they'd done to hurt her. And she eventually married a wonderful man and had two children—a son and a daughter.

Maybe you're like Winnie. You've come from a broken home. You're struggling to forgive the ones who caused the chaos. Today is a good day to let go of the pain of the past and focus on the family God has placed you in, right here, right now.

Forgive. Let go. Then watch as God brings new hope for better days ahead.

Father, I choose today to forgive all those who have hurt me,
either on purpose or by accident. I release them and
ask for You to give me a fresh start. Amen.—JT

FORGIVEN—
WHAT A TESTIMONY!

Come and hear, all you who fear God,
and I will declare what He has done for my soul.
PSALM 66:16 NKJV

Mariah knew what it was like to live behind bars. She'd spent the last six years in a shared cell, wondering when—or if—she would ever have a normal life again. When release day came at last, she walked out into the sunshine, her heart in her throat.

Now what? Could she really learn to live in freedom without reverting to her old ways? Would she make new friends and develop new habits? With determination leading the way, she took necessary steps. Mariah joined a 12-step program. She started attending church. She stayed away from the people who would drag her down. In short, she made up her mind to begin again.

Maybe you've never been confined to a prison cell but you've known the pain of living a life confined by sin or addiction. Today, like Mariah, you can step outside the imprisonment of those bars and live a life of freedom and victory. It won't be easy. You'll have to make tough choices. But if you're willing to accept God's forgiveness, then permanent, eternal freedom can be yours. You'll truly be made new, the past in the past. . .forever.

Father, I love Your version of freedom! Thank You
for shaking those prison bars and setting me free.
I step out into my new life today, Lord. Amen.—JT

AMAZING GRACE

Because of our faith, Christ has brought us into this place of
undeserved privilege where we now stand, and we confidently
and joyfully look forward to sharing God's glory.

ROMANS 5:2 NLT

Perhaps you've sung the old hymn "Amazing Grace." The melody is breathtaking and the lyrics offer a compelling reminder that the Lord's grace toward us, even when we sin, is beyond our comprehension. The work of Jesus on the cross provides humankind with the finest gift anyone could ever receive.

No one understood this better than the author of the hymn, John Newton. A slave owner and sailor in the Royal Navy, Newton experienced a radical transformation in his life. He fought to end slavery in England, which remained a bitter battle until the end.

Newton came to understand that his own sins—though they were many—were forgiven because of Christ's amazing grace. Jesus paid a remarkable price for that grace, His very life. Newton saw this grace as a divine miracle, and indeed, it is!

Have you experienced God's amazing grace? Have you asked Him to wash you clean from your sins? If so, then you can experience the divine miracle just like John Newton. Don't wait. Today is your day.

Father, it's Your amazing grace that saved me.
How I praise You for such a gift. Amen.—JT

BELIEVE TO RECEIVE

"If you believe, you will receive whatever you ask for in prayer."
MATTHEW 21:22 NIV

Picture yourself on your birthday. A friend is handing you a wrapped gift, one with your name on it. You want to take it, to open it, to share the excitement of your special day. But something keeps you from doing so. Instead, you set the gift on the table and stare at it, and then you take it home and stare at it some more.

A few days later your friend asks, "What did you think of the gift?"

"Oh, it's lovely," you say. "Thanks so much." But you don't really know if it's truly lovely, do you? You never actually opened the package.

That's how it is for some people when they come to know the Lord. They accept the gift of salvation, but all of the other things that come with it—joy, peace, hope, and so on? They completely overlook those.

God wants you to open the whole package. He longs for you to experience the joy of knowing Him fully. Today, open your eyes to the wonder of knowing and loving God in His fullness. Then celebrate those gifts by opening every package, one by one.

Lord, thank You for the gifts that come with
salvation and forgiveness. I'm so grateful
for all You've given me. Amen.–JT

PERFECT IN WEAKNESS

*And He said to me, "My grace is sufficient for you,
for My strength is made perfect in weakness." Therefore
most gladly I will rather boast in my infirmities, that the
power of Christ may rest upon me. Therefore I take pleasure
in infirmities, in reproaches, in needs, in persecutions, in
distresses, for Christ's sake. For when I am weak, then I am strong.*

2 CORINTHIANS 12:9–10 NKJV

The disciple Peter walked and talked with Jesus for over three years. He was blessed to know Jesus as both friend and Savior. Peter knew Him, loved Him, cared deeply about serving and worshipping Him. But when it came right down to it, in his hour of temptation, he chose to deny his best friend—not once, but three times. Peter quickly caved in and continued to fall deeper into the hole, until he finally felt there was no way out.

Jesus not only forgave Peter but gave him the opportunity—three times over—to redeem himself. And He's just as gracious with you. Even if you've turned your back on Him, He won't turn His back on you. The forgiveness of Jesus is yours for the asking. Take a lesson from Peter and return to the Lord if you've wandered away. His forgiveness is free and is offered from a heart of deep love to you, His child.

*Lord, I've failed You so many times. I'm so grateful for
Your forgiveness. Today I accept it freely. Amen.—JT*

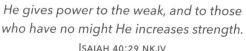

POWER BOOST

He gives power to the weak, and to those
who have no might He increases strength.
ISAIAH 40:29 NKJV

Remember the old cartoon *Popeye the Sailor Man*? Popeye was a typical guy, a bit on the wimpy side, even, until he ate his spinach. As soon as he swallowed down that can of greens, supernatural things started happening. Muscles popped out! He gained immediate strength. Just one can of spinach and Popeye was stronger, tougher, more capable. He could take down foes, stand up to enemies, and accomplish supernatural tasks for the good of mankind.

Think about that can of spinach as it relates to your spiritual life. God didn't save you so that you would live a wimpy life. You've been forgiven so that you can perform Popeye-like feats. When you swallow down God's Word (it's filled with supernatural nutrients), you get the energy you need to go above and beyond, to have power beyond your wildest imaginings. The past doesn't hold you bound when you receive forgiveness from your Creator. You're freed up to do. . .and be.

You're just like Popeye, sister! Enjoy your new life—forgiven, free, and strong in Him.

Thank You for giving me supernatural strength, Lord. I feel Your
supernatural power flowing through my veins. Your forgiveness
has set me free to do amazing things for You. Amen.—JT

CONFIRMED BY THE WORD

So faith comes from hearing, that is,
hearing the Good News about Christ.
ROMANS 10:17 NLT

Aren't you glad your salvation isn't based on your emotions? Whew! What a mess that would be! Up one day and down the next, you would be questioning your relationship with Jesus every day! That's no way to live.

Christ came to save you for all eternity, not just on the days when you're feeling spiritual. He took your emotions into consideration when He worked out your salvation. The goodness of God, the kindness of His nature, means you don't have to continually ask, "Did He really forgive me? I'm just not feeling it today."

He did forgive you, once and for all. So on those days when you're "feeling" otherwise, turn to His Word. Memorize the verses that give you assurance of your salvation. Take them to heart. Remind yourself that feelings are fleeting and often deceptive. If your salvation depended on your feelings, then what role would the cross play? Truly, the death of Jesus on the cross and His resurrection three days later sealed the deal. There's nothing more you need to do, other than to believe in Him and accept that free gift.

I'm so glad You don't base my salvation on my emotions,
Lord. Your gift of forgiveness is free to me, but it cost
You everything! How I praise You! Amen.—JT

FORGIVEN TO SERVE

You, my brothers and sisters, were called to be free.
But do not use your freedom to indulge the flesh;
rather, serve one another humbly in love.

GALATIANS 5:13 NIV

Perhaps you've never heard the name Lottie Moon. This precious woman was a missionary to China from the late 1800s to the early 1900s. Though short in stature, she stood heads above those around her spiritually. Lottie was raised in church, but it didn't really "take." It wasn't until she went through a spiritual awakening on her college campus that she came alive for Jesus. She accepted His free gift of salvation, applied His forgiveness to her life, and was never the same. She went on to do great things for the kingdom of God.

Lottie recognized something very important—forgiveness leads to service. When you've been forgiven, you have a greater capacity to serve. Your heart is so full of gratitude for what the Lord has done for you, you want to give back. This realization gave Lottie the nudge she needed to serve God on the mission field.

Isn't that how you felt after Jesus forgave you? You want to do great things for Him. Oh, the places you'll go when you're walking a fully forgiven life.

Thank You for saving me to serve, Jesus. I love sharing
my gifts for the benefit of Your kingdom. Amen.—JT

WALK BY FAITH

For we walk by faith, not by sight.
2 CORINTHIANS 5:7 ESV

If you've read John Bunyan's wonderful classic, *Pilgrim's Progress*, you know that Pilgrim (who's representative of everyman) is on a faith journey to the Celestial City (symbolic of heaven). He encounters many people along the way and struggles with his faith as the journey progresses.

Pilgrim's faith-walk is a tough one, just as the modern-day Christian's faith-walk tends to be. That's why the Bible encourages us to walk by faith and not by sight. If we spent too much time looking at the issues going on around us, we would be completely overwhelmed and discouraged. It would stop us in our tracks and we'd never get anything done.

Lift your eyes, Pilgrim! Be reminded of who you are and *whose* you are. Jesus gave you new life and set you on this journey so that you could develop your relationship with Him and point others toward heaven while doing so. Sure, there will be obstacles. Yes, you'll have bumps in the road. But don't give up. Keep trekking forward, your vision squarely on Him. Let faith be your guide, and—whatever you do—don't look back.

Father, I get it. This journey is meant to be an adventure.
I'll keep moving forward with Your help, Lord. Amen.–JT

SET YOUR MIND ON THINGS ABOVE

For to set the mind on the flesh is death, but to
set the mind on the Spirit is life and peace.
ROMANS 8:6 ESV

Jillian had a tendency to stress out. . .a lot. Instead of trusting God, she often put her trust in her own goals, dreams, and aspirations. This tendency led to many years of chaos and confusion. She would make up her mind about something one minute then shift in a completely different direction the next. Over and over again she would change her mind. She just couldn't seem to figure out a straight path toward her goals.

When you set your mind on earthly things, you often end up confused, just like Jillian. Whatever feels good or right in the moment is what you chase after. The problem with chasing earthly goals or treasures is that they fluctuate all the time.

God wants you to chase after Him, nothing else. The only way you can do that is to set your thoughts—your mind—on things above, not on the things of this world. Begin to care more about the Lord's opinion than the things you want in this life. Be reminded of all He's done for you already. If He saved you, giving you new life in Him, you can surely trust Him with all the rest.

Thank You for the reminder that I need to set my mind on
things above, Lord! I will follow hard after You. Amen.–JT

FORGIVEN TO FORGIVE

Instead, be kind to each other, tenderhearted, forgiving one another, just as God through Christ has forgiven you.
EPHESIANS 4:32 NLT

One thing about the forgiveness of God. . .it causes you to be much more forgiving of others. Sure, there will be people who are difficult to forgive–those who hurt you on purpose, for instance. But when God is in it, you can forgive even the vilest person.

If anyone knew what it was like to have to forgive the unforgivable, it was Elisabeth Elliot, wife of missionary Jim Elliot. His life was taken by members of the Auca tribe (a native tribe from Ecuador) while he was trying to share the Gospel. Elisabeth was devastated. It seemed impossible to forgive the men who had taken the love of her life and the father of her only daughter.

Over a period of years, she not only forgave the men who killed her husband but actually led them to the Lord. Elisabeth ended up ministering to the tribal people and shared the love of Jesus with them. Before long, the very men who had killed Jim were counted among her friends.

That's what forgiveness does: it frees you up to forgive others, even the ones you're sure you'll never be able to forgive.

Lord, there are probably a few people in my life I need to forgive, even now. If You could forgive me, Father, I will make the choice to forgive them. Thank You for the reminder. Amen.–JT

LOVING LARGE

"Therefore I tell you, her sins, which are many, are forgiven—for she loved much. But he who is forgiven little, loves little."

LUKE 7:47 ESV

Don't you love this verse from Luke chapter 7? When you've lived a rough life, when your sins have been many, you appreciate the grace and mercy of the Lord so much. It seems almost impossible that God could forgive you for the things you've done, but He has. And because you're so grateful, you learn to love and forgive others to that same degree.

Sometimes, though, to those who carry a bit of a holier-than-thou attitude, the ability to extend grace and mercy doesn't come as easily. Perhaps they don't see themselves as having been much in need of a Savior. Or maybe they've just forgotten the great lengths God went to in order to draw them to Him.

No matter where you've come from, no matter how great or small your sins have been, learn to love much. Let go of that holier-than-thou attitude. Forgive much. Offer grace as often as you can. In doing so, you'll be reminded of all that God has done in your own life.

Father, I will do my best to love much! You've forgiven me time and time again. How could I stop short of forgiving others? Amen.—JT

HOLY BANKING

*"And forgive us our debts, as we
also have forgiven our debtors."*
MATTHEW 6:12 NIV

Marigold knew what it felt like to have a debt forgiven. On the week of her wedding, her father stepped in and paid off her student loans so that she and her husband could enter their marriage debt free. The relief was immediate and overwhelming.

Maybe you've had a debt relieved too. Or maybe you've paid off a loan that long plagued you. Doesn't it feel good not to owe anyone? That's what it's like for the believer when they accept the price that Jesus paid on the cross. The debt is paid in full. There's no balance on the loan. The account is closed, once and for all.

God's banking system works in your favor, for sure. When your account is paid off, you're freed up to forgive others for the sins they've committed against you. When you live in a way that brings glory to God, everyone wins. You can take that to the bank!

*Father, I love Your system of banking.
My account is paid in full. You paid the
price for my sin, and I'm so grateful. Amen.—JT*

BEARING ONE ANOTHER UP

*Bearing with one another and, if one has a complaint
against another, forgiving each other; as the Lord
has forgiven you, so you also must forgive.*
COLOSSIANS 3:13 ESV

Have you ever watched a high-rise building go up? It's fascinating to see the framework, isn't it? (And it's a little terrifying to see the workers perched atop that framework!) Without that solid frame, one floor could not sit atop another. The whole thing would crumble. One floor depends upon another.

The same is true in our spiritual walk. In many ways, forgiveness is the framework that strengthens our lives. It's the unseen force holding the building up. Without it, the whole thing would come tumbling down to the ground below.

God wants you to be solid in your faith. Accept His forgiveness. Enjoy it. Think about it. Talk about it. Share what He's done so that others can be made strong as well. And while you're at it, don't hold grudges against those who've hurt you. Bear them up, even when they've injured you. Bolster the framework of their lives so that they too can live in freedom.

*Lord, I want to be strong in You. Your forgiveness
bears me up, and I, in turn, will strengthen others
by offering them forgiveness too. Amen.–JT*

HOLD TRUE

Only let us hold true to what we have attained.
PHILIPPIANS 3:16 ESV

Picture a boat attached to its moorings. A storm hits, one with howling winds. It whips the waves into a fury, causing the boat to rock to and fro. If it isn't tied down securely, the boat will break loose and float out to sea, where it will likely be destroyed.

The same is true with believers who don't stay grounded in Christ. Even though they've been forgiven and set free, some find their walk with Jesus too confining or too difficult. The temptation to go back to the past is as strong as the pull of those storm gales. So they break free and do their own thing for a while. Before long, ocean waves crash in a tempest around them and reality sets in. Without their moorings, safety is a thing of the past. Unattached to shore, they are doomed to sink.

Once you've been set free from sin, don't give in to the temptation to return to it. Stay tethered to the Lord, even if it seems the more difficult choice. In the end, remaining close to Him will make you stronger, safer, and—ultimately—happier.

Lord, I will stay tethered to You. No matter
how tough life gets, I won't let go. Amen.–JT

FRESH MERCY

The faithful love of the LORD never ends! His mercies never cease. Great is his faithfulness; his mercies begin afresh each morning.
LAMENTATIONS 3:22–23 NLT

The Israelites left Egypt headed for the Promised Land. Along the way, God performed numerous miracles for them. He split the Red Sea so they could walk across on dry land, met Moses on the mountain to give His commandments, and even sent water from a rock.

The Lord did something else for His children too. Every morning dew would settle on the ground. When it evaporated, something appeared underneath. Manna. Bread from heaven. This heavenly provision was hidden under the dew. The Israelites might have missed it if they hadn't waited for the dew to dissipate.

God's mercies are just like that dew. They appear fresh and new every morning. And if you're patient, if you're paying attention, you'll see that something remarkable lies beneath the surface. There are hidden blessings in those mercies. Love. Joy. Peace. Forgiveness. Longsuffering. You name it, you'll find it when you find Him.

Thank You, Jesus, that Your mercies are new every morning. They sustain me. They give me life, just like the manna nourished the Israelites. I'm so grateful, Lord. Amen.—JT

FORGIVEN FOR GOOD WORKS

Command them to do good, to be rich in good deeds,
and to be generous and willing to share.
1 TIMOTHY 6:18 NIV

If you've seen *The Wizard of Oz*, you probably remember the scene where the Tin Man approaches the wizard asking for a heart. The wizard can't offer him a real heart, but gives the Tin Man a heart-shaped watch that makes a ticking sound. He goes on to explain that even people with far less heart than the Tin Man can perform good deeds. He calls them "good deed doers."

The truth is, the Tin Man always had a heart. The scarecrow always had a brain. The lion always had courage. What they lacked was the "oomph" behind their gifts, the spark to ignite them, to set them in action.

You've been given many good gifts too. And when you come to Christ, when you are born again—forgiven and set free from the past—He lights the spark that stirs up those gifts once and for all. In that moment, the Holy Spirit invigorates you, setting you on fire to do great things.

Lord, I'm so grateful for the spark of Your forgiveness.
Thank You for giving me the "oomph" that stirs up my gifts,
allowing me to serve others and You. Amen.—JT

FORGIVEN TO LIVE IN JOY

Rejoice in the Lord always; again I will say, rejoice.

PHILIPPIANS 4:4 ESV

There are many joyful people in the world, but some seem to effervesce with more bubbles than others. What makes them so special? What sets them apart?

Forgiveness is the great motivator that frees people up to live in God-breathed joy. When you've been set free from bondage, loosed from the chains of sin, you're free to step into a new existence, out of darkness and into His marvelous light.

When that happens, you have so much to be grateful for, you just can't help yourself. Joy bubbles up inside of you as your heart bursts into a song of celebration: "I'm set free! I'm a child of the King!"

Where are you on the joy meter today? Are you half full? Completely full? Let the Lord remind you of all He's accomplished in your heart. As you realize the depth of His great love for you, bubbles will rise to the surface. You won't be able to help yourself. Your joy will be contagious to all you come in contact with.

Lord, today I feel like I'm bubbling over with joy.
You've given me so much. How can I ever repay You?
Thank You for setting me free, Father. Amen.—JT

ARMS SPREAD WIDE

As far as the east is from the west, so far has
He removed our transgressions from us.
PSALM 103:12 NKJV

He hung on the cross, the pain with each breath more agonizing than the breath before. The thief looked to his left at the man they called Jesus. A crowd had gathered around, many weeping for Him. What would it be like, the thief wondered, to be adored like that? Yet just as many jeered at Jesus, calling Him names and accusing Him of being a blasphemer.

Still, there was something about this man. It was undeniable. The thief spoke from his heart, each word causing pain as it escaped: "Remember me when you come into Your kingdom!" Jesus turned to him, eyes filled with love, and responded, "Today you will be with Me in paradise."

Suddenly the pain lifted. His imminent death no longer mattered. Today he would be with Jesus. . .in paradise. Was such a thing really possible?

The same gift that Jesus offered the thief that day is offered freely to you. Life eternal. It comes from One with arms stretched wide, One willing to remove your sin as far as the east is from the west.

Lord, I thank You for Your work on the cross.
It has truly changed everything. Amen.–JT

THE DEPTHS OF THE SEA

You will again have compassion on us; you will tread our sins underfoot and hurl all our iniquities into the depths of the sea.
MICAH 7:19 NIV

Think about the *Titanic* as it sank to the bottom of the sea. What once was grand and glorious is now hidden forever, buried in the depths of the ocean. That mighty ship is gone forever, wedged deep into the sandy floor of the sea.

Today's scripture from the book of Micah assures us that God's anger doesn't last forever. (Aren't you glad about that?) He releases it, offers forgiveness, and casts our sin into the sea, where it sinks in *Titanic* fashion to the depths, gone forever.

Wouldn't it be fun to watch God "cast" your sin? What do you suppose that would look like? Think about the pitcher from your favorite baseball team. Before he pitches the ball, he pulls his arm back in preparation so that it will sail faster, farther, and with more precision. Now picture God taking all of the awful things you've done, pulling back His arm, and hurling them into the sea. (No wonder they hit the bottom–He's got quite an arm!)

What an amazing, forgiving God we serve.

Lord, thank You for casting my sin far, far away.
I'm so glad I'll never see it again! Amen.–JT

SET ON YOU

You will keep in perfect peace all who trust in you,
all whose thoughts are fixed on you!
ISAIAH 26:3 NLT

When you were a child, did you ever play the staring game with a friend? The goal of the game was to keep gazing into each other's eyes without blinking. The first to blink lost the game. It wasn't always easy, but you did your best not to shift your gaze.

In much the same way, God wants you to keep your focus riveted on Him. Don't get distracted, looking to the right or the left. Remain fixed on Him. Sure, there will be plenty of opportunities to shift your gaze. Distractions will come in varying forms and fashions, many of them calling out to you. "Look this way!" "Pay attention to me, not what God has to say!"

Don't be fooled. It's not what's in your peripheral vision that propels you forward, after all. Your heart will follow what you fully see. God wants to be seen. When your vision remains fixed on Him, your heart is set, your steps secure, and your future bright.

Lord, I will set my eyes on You. I won't look back to the sins of yesterday. I won't look ahead to the worries of tomorrow. I'll fasten my gaze on You, the author and finisher of my faith. Amen.—JT

FORGIVEN TO DO GREAT THINGS

Commit to the LORD whatever you do,
and he will establish your plans.
PROVERBS 16:3 NIV

The great Scottish missionary and physician David Livingstone was used greatly by God. A pioneer missionary, explorer, and anti-slavery crusader, he became something of a legend. Stories about him continue, nearly 150 years after his death.

In examining the life of this great man, several questions have to be asked: What propelled him to go to Africa in the first place? Why did he feel the need to leave all he knew and loved to go so far away? And after facing the many struggles he had while in Africa, what propelled him to stay?

Here's the truth: God offers forgiveness and salvation so that we are freed up to do amazing things for Him. Perhaps you won't be a David Livingstone. You won't travel to distant shores or risk your life to share the Gospel message. That's not the point. The Lord can (and will) still use you to accomplish great things for the kingdom of God.

What adventures do you see on the horizon? Aren't you glad He has saved you, delivered you, and set you free so that you can step out into all He has planned for you?

Lord, thank You for putting me on an adventurous path.
Like David Livingstone, I want to do amazing things
for You. Let the journey begin! Amen.—JT

SHARPENED BY THE WORD

For the word of God is living and active, sharper than any two-edged sword, piercing to the division of soul and of spirit, of joints and of marrow, and discerning the thoughts and intentions of the heart.

HEBREWS 4:12 ESV

Have you ever worked with a dull knife? Maybe you needed to cut through a freshly baked loaf of bread or a savory rib eye steak. Only the knife barely made a dent, so you found yourself sawing back and forth, eventually giving up.

The Word of God isn't dull, not by any stretch of the imagination. It'll slice through and leave a clean mark. When you allow it to do its work, you'll find yourself challenged, changed, and hopeful. If you dull yourself to it, you will find that you are weak, wishy-washy, and lacking motivation.

What scriptures motivate you? Are there any particular verses that cut through your struggles, your addictions, and your pain? Allow God to use His Word to do a deep work. Don't settle for a mediocre lifestyle. Go all the way with your daily Bible time–from forgiveness of sins to the honing of your gifts. Let the Word do its complete work.

Lord, I trust Your Word to cut through the chaos of my life and bring clean, sharp edges. I submit myself to the process. Amen.–JT

BEARING REBUKE

"So watch yourselves! If another believer sins, rebuke that person; then if there is repentance, forgive. Even if that person wrongs you seven times a day and each time turns again and asks forgiveness, you must forgive."

LUKE 17:3-4 NLT

Yvonne had a hard time taking critique. . .from anyone. She got rankled whenever her boss would correct mistakes at work. Even her friends walked on eggshells around her, worried they would hurt her feelings. When she did get her feelings hurt, she was hard pressed to forgive. Instead, she seemed to bottle up her emotions and get more bitter with time.

People like Yvonne often have a hard time giving and accepting grace. They struggle to see the value in change. Maybe you can relate. Perhaps you're opposed to the idea of receiving critique because you know it might force you to face the truth—that there are areas of your life in need of tweaking. You simply don't want to hear it, so you close your ears to it.

God didn't forgive you to leave you stuck in a rut. He wants you to change and grow over time. So open your heart, mind, and ears to a little bit of critique every now and again. Don't take it personally. Don't feel wounded. Just take the advice that makes sense, toss the rest, and grow in grace.

Thanks for the reminder that I don't have to let critique wound me, Lord. I want to grow, grow, grow. Amen.–JT

FORGIVEN TO SET AN EXAMPLE

*Don't let anyone look down on you because you
are young, but set an example for the believers
in speech, in conduct, in love, in faith and in purity.*

1 TIMOTHY 4:12 NIV

Moses was a man who learned how to reinvent himself. He was born a slave, but a series of fascinating events led him to the palace. Raised in opulence, he seemed to be set for life. But God had other ideas. He called Moses out of his comfort zone and instructed him to lead the Israelites out of Egypt, out of bondage and into freedom. Talk about a change of pace!

God has done the same for you. He's led you out of the bondage of sin and into complete freedom in Christ by offering forgiveness and salvation. And God is using you, like Moses, to set an example for those around you. You're not leading thousands of people across the desert toward the Promised Land, but in a way, you are leading people toward a relationship with Christ, which will get them to the ultimate promised land, heaven.

You were forgiven and set free so that you could reach others. What a blessing to know that God can use you to guide others to Him. When you get to heaven, imagine your joy at seeing all the people who followed your lead.

*Lord, I want to be the best example I
can be. Help me, I pray. Amen.–JT*

CONFESSION

*Whoever conceals his transgressions will not prosper,
but he who confesses and forsakes them will obtain mercy.*
PROVERBS 28:13 ESV

From the time Deborah was a little girl, she had a hard time coming clean when she messed up, even when caught in the act. Instead of just saying, "You're right. I did that. I'm sorry," she would argue and debate. She didn't seem to see her own flaws or mistakes.

Jump ahead into adulthood. The misguided belief that she was rarely wrong spilled over into Deborah's work life and caused problems with coworkers. It also created grief at home. Her husband didn't care much for the notion that he was always the one to blame.

It wasn't until people started pulling away from Deborah that she was forced to face the truth. She needed to confess her wrongdoings to the Lord (and several loved ones, friends, and coworkers as well) and then ask for forgiveness. Deborah was startled at the responses of those she'd hurt. Instead of getting angry, most were thrilled to hear her admission of guilt. The heartfelt words shared between them reestablished relationships and made her more vulnerable.

Take a lesson from Deborah. Confess your faults to your loved ones. God will help you. "Confession is good for the soul" is more than just a saying. Confession can change (and even save) your life.

*Father, today I come to You to share the
things I've done wrong. I need Your
forgiveness, Lord. Amen.—JT*

HIS LOVE CHANGES EVERYTHING

"For God so loved the world, that he gave
his only Son, that whoever believes in him
should not perish but have eternal life."
JOHN 3:16 ESV

No doubt you've heard (and quoted) John 3:16 many times over. It's the most-loved verse in the Bible, after all. God loved mankind so much that He gave—not just His love, His joy, His peace, His forgiveness—but the very One who mattered most to Him, His Son. And He didn't just give His Son for people who had their act together. Jesus came to save the lost, no matter how devious or deadly their behavior.

Perhaps no biblical hero personifies this better than the apostle Paul. Before he came to know Jesus, Paul was a persecutor of Christians. He loved nothing more than exposing and punishing them. Paul was a bad dude. But Jesus died for Paul too. . .just like He died for the sins of all of us.

If God could forgive a man who persecuted believers, then He can forgive you. If He can take Paul's evil mindset and turn it to good, then imagine what He'll do for that friend or loved one you're praying for.

God loves. . .and His love changes everything.

Lord, if You can grant forgiveness and restoration
to a man like Paul, then I know You can change
my loved one too. I'm so grateful! Amen.—JT

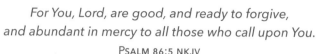

ABOUNDING LOVE

For You, Lord, are good, and ready to forgive,
and abundant in mercy to all those who call upon You.
PSALM 86:5 NKJV

Can you imagine how difficult things would be if you had to walk around in condemnation all the time? What would your life be like if you'd never been given an opportunity to let go of the past? If you couldn't move forward without feeling guilty about every little thing you'd done, would you still be the person you are today? (No doubt you're shuddering, just thinking about how different things would be!)

God's free gift of salvation is far more than a "get into heaven free" card. It's a "celebrate life to the fullest here on earth" card as well. It's an assurance that you're loved, cared for, wanted, accepted, and fully forgiven, no matter what you've done. Salvation is love, wrapped up in a story of life, death on a cross, and resurrection power.

Let's face it—everyone wants to feel loved. Everyone wants to feel accepted. The body of Christ is here for people, no matter their background, no matter the person they used to be. God's love abounds toward us, and in turn our love abounds toward others, even those who've had serious struggles.

Thank You, Lord, that I don't have to walk around
feeling guilty about every little thing. You've freed me
up to live a full life, one where I can share Your amazing
love with people I meet along the way. Amen.—JT

ALL BOASTING ASIDE

*God saved you by his grace when you believed. And you
can't take credit for this; it is a gift from God. Salvation is
not a reward for the good things we have done,
so none of us can boast about it.*

EPHESIANS 2:8–9 NLT

Have you ever met a braggart? They are thrilled to tell you of all their achievements—their elevated status at work, the amazing things they've accomplished, and the accolades they've received. You'd be hard pressed to get a word in edgewise with one of these folks because they're so busy singing their own praises.

God's Word makes it plain that we're not supposed to puff ourselves up, primarily because all that is good within us actually comes from the Lord, not ourselves. And also, being self-absorbed, self-focused, is a big turnoff to people. If you're trying to win others to the Lord, that's not the way to do it.

Put all boasting aside. You didn't forgive yourself. You didn't save yourself. You didn't die so that mankind could live. Shift your boasting to the Lord. Sing His praises, that all would come to know Him. Now that's a boast worth listening to!

*Lord, help me not to boast about my own
accomplishments. I want to stay focused on You
so that all will hear of Your great fame! Amen.–JT*

FORGIVEN TO LIVE FOREVER

*And this is the promise that
he made to us—eternal life.*
1 JOHN 2:25 ESV

Have you fully contemplated the word *eternity*? Doesn't it boggle your mind to know that, as a believer, as a child who has been fully forgiven, you will live forever and ever? (How long is forever, anyway?)

God's idea of time isn't like ours at all. It has no beginning and no end. The Bible says that, to the Lord, a thousand years is like a day and a day is like a thousand years (2 Peter 3:8). When we get to heaven, God won't be sitting on His throne with a watch in hand, keeping an eye on the minute or second hand. All of our watches and clocks will be tossed into the great abyss, never to be seen or heard from again.

God has placed eternity in your heart (Ecclesiastes 3:11). He longs for you to look at every situation you're currently facing with an eternal mindset. Don't fret over the non-eternal things. They will soon be gone in a mist, replaced with the joy of heaven.

Lord, thank You for the reminder that I don't have to worry about the non-eternal things. I'll be spending forever and ever with You. All that will matter then is my relationship with You. Amen.—JT

WONDERFUL PEACE

*"I have told you these things, so that in me you may
have peace. In this world you will have trouble.
But take heart! I have overcome the world."*

JOHN 16:33 NIV

Lanelle had a hard time finding peace in the middle of the storms of her life. She found herself knotted up much of the time. When things at work would go wrong, anxiety would get the best of her. And when relationships began to crumble, she completely fell apart.

It took some time for Lanelle to realize that peace—true and lasting peace—came from a deep, abiding relationship with the Lord. Without His forgiveness, His leading, His input, she would continue to overthink every situation and fret unnecessarily.

Maybe you struggle like Lanelle. You have a difficult time experiencing true peace. Today, give your heart fully and completely to the Lord. Allow Him to wash away the pain and the sins of yesterday. Put it all behind you, once and for all. Shaking off the remnants of your former life will prepare you to receive God-breathed peace, the kind you can't drum up on your own. And walking in that peace will bring great comfort and joy.

*Thank You, Lord, that I don't have to fret. Once I'm Your child,
You give me true and lasting peace. I praise You! Amen.—JT*

OUR MERCIFUL FATHER

"For I will be merciful toward their iniquities,
and I will remember their sins no more."
HEBREWS 8:12 ESV

Shonda was raised by parents who took her to church every Sunday. She was a consummate Sunday school kid, one who memorized the Bible verses and even won the annual Bible quiz. But something changed when she reached her teen years. Instead of seeing church as a place of excitement and growth, Shonda began to view it as boring and constrictive.

Oh, she kept going. Her parents made sure of that. But her behavior got riskier and more outlandish all the while. She developed an interest in the opposite sex early on, and the boys (even the ones at church) were happy to take a sabbatical from their Bible teaching long enough to engage in promiscuous behavior with Shonda.

Her teens and twenties were rough, in part because the promiscuity continued, and in part because she eventually left the church and had no one to hold her accountable. It wasn't until years later that the Lord finally wooed her back. When that happened, she prayed for a fresh start and God healed her of the pain of the past. He also restored her to the church and she found peace and solace there. He will do the same for you, no matter where you are in your journey. Head home. . .to the church and to Him.

Lord, I'm so glad You are wooing
Your children home! Amen.–JT

FORGIVEN TO HOLD ON

So let's not get tired of doing what is good.
At just the right time we will reap a harvest
of blessing if we don't give up.
GALATIANS 6:9 NLT

Have you ever watched a dog with a bone? He takes it very seriously, even when he's not chewing on it. Many times he'll hold it in his mouth, even when he's half-asleep. And if another dog comes along, watch out! Fido will fight to the death to keep that other canine from stealing his prized bone!

God wants us to hold on to our faith like a dog holds on to his bone. He wants us to be just as tenacious, just as determined, just as energetic. He longs for us to take it seriously, to guard it with our very lives. No matter what comes along to steal our faith, we can hold fast, just like Fido.

How are you doing with your faith? God didn't bring you this far to leave you hanging. He forgave you and set you free from the sins of yesterday to give you abundant life. So hang tight. Don't let go, even if you're growing weary. You will surely reap a reward if you don't give up.

Lord, I'm going to hold tight to my faith. I won't let
anyone—or anything—steal it from me. Amen.—JT

THE FORMER THINGS

"Forget the former things;
do not dwell on the past."
ISAIAH 43:18 NIV

Picture a glass of water. It's completely clear with no impurities at all. Now envision a drop of red food coloring being released into it. Everything changes. Imagine you add a drop of blue. The color changes again. On and on you go, adding a drip of this or a drop of that. Before long, you're left with a glass of gray, murky water, something you'd never feel comfortable drinking, thanks to all of the impurities.

That's how sin looks when it enters our lives. A little drop of this, a little drip of that, and before long things are looking gray and murky. That's why God longs for us to be forgiven and set free. And once we're free, He wants us to be "free indeed"—unwilling to focus on the past. Why? Because every time we move backward in our thoughts, it's like adding another drop to the glass again.

Today, make a decision to live a crystal-clear life, free from impurities. Don't let your thoughts travel backward. Be diligent about your thought-life. Don't let your mind wander back to yesterday. "Forget the former things." They are of no value to you now.

Lord, I will set my thoughts on You, not on my past.
Give me a crystal-clear thought-life, I pray. Amen.—JT

FORGIVEN. . .AND RIGHTEOUS

*If we confess our sins, he is faithful and just to forgive us
our sins and to cleanse us from all unrighteousness.*
1 JOHN 1:9 ESV

It was a simple mistake. She overslept and missed an important meeting at work, one her supervisor had arranged weeks ago. Tiana needed the forgiveness of her boss, but wondered if he would give it. He was a harsh man, not inclined to overlook mistakes. In the end, he made an example of her in front of her coworkers in a way that embarrassed and upset her. Things eventually calmed down, but not before she was made to look like a fool.

Aren't you glad God isn't like Tiana's boss? He's not interested in humiliating you when you've made a mistake. He won't make a big deal of it in front of others when you slip up. He simply offers to wash away the embarrassment and pain and give you a zillion chances to get it right next time.

Mistakes happen. You'll mess up on many, many occasions. But remember, your very gracious heavenly Father isn't standing over you with a stick in His hand, ready to give you a swat. Instead, His arms are open wide and He whispers, "It's okay, I forgive you," then restores you completely.

*Lord, I'm so glad You don't get angry when I mess up.
(You'd be angry a lot!) Thank You for forgiving me and
giving me chance after chance to get it right. Amen.—JT*

THE ULTIMATE GIFT CARD

*For he has rescued us from the kingdom of darkness
and transferred us into the Kingdom of his dear Son,
who purchased our freedom and forgave our sins.*
COLOSSIANS 1:13-14 NLT

Have you ever received a gift card to your favorite store or restaurant? Maybe it arrived on your birthday or Christmas. Perhaps someone passed it your way as an unexpected thank-you gift. You could hardly wait to redeem it. At absolutely no cost to you, that card would purchase a lovely gift, something you would never consider purchasing for yourself otherwise. (Talk about a fun shopping spree—free money!)

God's free gift of salvation is a lot like that gift card. He has offered it at no cost to you, but there's a redemption process. You have to take the free gift He offers and apply it to your life. Once that is done, what a lovely gift you'll receive, the gift of salvation.

Today, take the time to thank God for the gift card He has handed to you. Take it in hand and enjoy the greatest gift you'll ever receive, one Someone else paid the ultimate price for—salvation!

*Thank You for the gift of salvation, Lord. What a
price You paid for my forgiveness. I willingly
accept this precious, holy gift! Amen.—JT*

BY HIS STRIPES

*But he was pierced for our transgressions; he was crushed
for our iniquities; upon him was the chastisement that
brought us peace, and with his wounds we are healed.*

ISAIAH 53:5 ESV

Shortly before His crucifixion, Jesus took a beating from the guards of Pontius Pilate. They gave him thirty-nine lashes. Every time that whip came down on His back, cutting through His flesh and leaving marks deep enough to cause severe anguish, something significant was happening. Your healing was being purchased.

It's so hard to picture the Savior of the world, the Creator of all, taking a beating so that you could have wholeness, but that's exactly what happened. By His stripes, we are healed. That's biblical truth, but it's hard for most of us to swallow. With His crushing, we are made whole. By His wounding, our transgressions are wiped clean. Through His death on the cross, forgiveness is ours.

He did it all out of great love for us. His pain bought our gain. His agony bought our joy. His stripes bought our healing. What a precious Savior!

*Lord, I don't know how I can ever repay You for all You've
done for me. I'm here today because of the work You did
on the cross. You've brought me peace, joy, and healing,
and I'm eternally grateful, Jesus! Amen.–JT*

FORGIVEN TO PRAISE

Through him then let us continually offer up a sacrifice of praise to God, that is, the fruit of lips that acknowledge his name.
HEBREWS 13:15 ESV

Can you imagine what praise-a-thons are going to be like in heaven? Gathered around the throne with all of God's kids—not just the ones who are living now but the apostles and believers from hundreds, even thousands of years back! How wonderful it will be. Can you even imagine the voices raised in chorus—perhaps in thousands of different languages at once?

You don't have to wait until you get to heaven to start praising Him. Jesus is worthy of your praise right here, right now. It's perfectly natural for a daughter of the Most High God to praise her Creator. In fact, His free gift of salvation should make your heart want to burst into song. When you think of all He's saved you from, joy abounds!

God forgave you and set you free from a life of bondage and pain. He offered forgiveness when you had no hope. That's an amazing gift worth celebrating! Don't be intimidated. Don't worry about what others are thinking when you lift your hands and heart to the King of kings. He's worthy of praise, after all!

Father, I'm so happy and grateful for all You've done. I don't want to wait for heaven to begin praise's song. I'll begin right now: You're so worthy, Lord! How I praise You! Amen.–JT

GOD'S HOLY PATIENCE

The Lord is not slow in keeping his promise,
as some understand slowness. Instead he is
patient with you, not wanting anyone to perish,
but everyone to come to repentance.

2 PETER 3:9 NIV

If you've ever walked a toddler through his twos and threes, you've definitely earned multiple stars in your heavenly crown. Little ones in that age group can try your patience, for sure. From shouting "No!" to hitting, biting, and slapping. . .two- and three-year-olds can perplex you with a host of antics. And often, despite your best attempts, they refuse to be tamed.

Now think about how many times God has had to exhibit that same patience with you. Surely you've tried His patience a time or two as well! Oh, maybe you're not hitting, biting, or slapping, but perhaps you've hit someone below the belt with a snarky comment or you've offered a biting critique to a loved one or coworker. The truth is, we're all toddlers at heart. Without the love and grace of Jesus, we'd all be untamable!

God's patience is remarkable, when you think about it like that. And He's never going to give up on you, no matter how you try that patience!

Thank You for Your patience, Lord! I'm sorry I've acted like
a temperamental toddler at times. I'm so grateful for the
many times You've brought gentle correction and
forgiveness. I've surely needed it. Amen.–JT

FEAR, BE GONE

For God has not given us a spirit of fear and timidity,
but of power, love, and self-discipline.
2 TIMOTHY 1:7 NLT

God offers His kids many gifts, but fear isn't one of them. If you're afraid, if you're struggling to get over the hurdle of fear, you can rest assured—it's not from God. The enemy of your soul is in the business of fear-mongering, but God never is. It's against His nature to inflict pain on His kids, after all.

What are you afraid of, even now? Bills? Finances? A work situation? A relational problem? Take it to God, the One who squelches every fear with His great love.

Maybe you're afraid that His work on the cross wasn't enough and that you're not really forgiven for the things you did in your former life. The memories haunt you and you secretly wonder if they're haunting God too.

It's impossible to fully understand the grace and mercy of God, but His forgiveness is real. . .and lasting. He forgave those things you did so long ago. He washed them away in the blood of His Son. Any fear related to the things you did once-upon-a-time has to go, in Jesus' name!

I give my fears and insecurities to You, Lord. You've already
forgiven me. I stand firm in that knowledge! Amen.–JT

FORGIVEN TO LOVE

*Above all, keep loving one another earnestly,
since love covers a multitude of sins.*

1 Peter 4:8 esv

She fought against the men as they dragged her through the crowd. The woman tried to cry out, but they refused to listen. What could she say, anyway? She'd been caught in the very act of adultery, after all. And now these religious zealots wanted to make sure she got the punishment she deserved.

They shoved her forward, to the feet of a man with nothing but kindness in His eyes. He turned to face her as her accusers cried out: "Stone her! Adulteress! Punish her!"

Through the din, she watched something remarkable. The stranger reached down and scribbled something in the sand with His fingertip. Then He looked up at her accusers and spoke with firmness: "Let him who is without sin cast the first stone."

The crowd began to back away. One by one, the zealots left, taking their accusations with them. When she found herself face-to-face with the kindhearted stranger, He looked at her with such love that her heart began to melt. "Where are your accusers now?" He asked. Then He spoke with tenderness: "Go and sin no more."

Jesus says the same thing to each of us. "Where are your accusers now?" No condemnation. Only love. And that love propels us to rise, as this precious woman did, and walk into a brand-new life.

*I have no accusers, Jesus. In You,
I am completely free! Amen.—JT*

WHILE WE WERE YET SINNERS

But God demonstrates His own love toward us, in that
while we were still sinners, Christ died for us.
ROMANS 5:8 NKJV

When did Jesus fall in love with you? Was it when you finally got your act together and decided to follow Him? Or did it happen earlier than that? Did He love you when you were a little kid, playing at your daddy's feet?

The truth is, God has loved you from the moment you were conceived in your mother's womb. He has never stopped loving you, even when you disobeyed your parents or wandered away from the things you knew to be right. The Lord's love traveled across multiple years and countless situations to cover you when you were on the run from Him. And that same love drew you back, finally winning your heart.

Knowing that love has changed you in a thousand ways. It has made you a better woman, a stronger person, and more vulnerable as well. You've experienced forgiveness, new life, and so much more. What a wonderful feeling, to be free and hopeful, ready to face a new day. And what a gracious God to offer such freedom while you were yet a sinner.

Thank You for giving me new chances even when I was on the
run from You, Lord. As broken and flawed as I was, You still
gave Your life for me, Jesus. I'm so grateful! Amen.–JT

STRENGTHENED TO FORGIVE

I can do all this through him who gives me strength.
PHILIPPIANS 4:13 NIV

If you're like most women, you pay attention to your diet. You do your best to eat not only foods that give you the nutrients you need, but foods that make you feel good from the inside out. You've come to understand that your health is one of the most important things to preserve, and you try to make good choices so that you can have a long, healthy life.

God does want you to be strong, but not just physically. He wants you to be even stronger spiritually. This starts with giving your heart to Him and accepting His free gift of salvation. From there, staying in His Word, spending time in prayer, and sharing your faith with others will beef you up, spiritually speaking.

One of the key benefits of being strong in Him is realizing that you can do all things through Him who strengthens you. You don't have to depend on yourself anymore. The very One who loved you, wooed you, forgave you, and offered you new life stands ready to work through you to do amazing things. It's not your strength, girl. It's His. Enjoy it!

I'm so glad You give me strength, Lord. I don't have
to depend on myself. You're working through
me even now. I'm so blessed! Amen.—JT

ABOUNDING IN HOPE

I pray that God, the source of hope, will fill you completely with joy and peace because you trust in him. Then you will overflow with confident hope through the power of the Holy Spirit.

ROMANS 15:13 NLT

Nina was one of those gals who was up one minute and down the next. She couldn't seem to control her emotions. She tended to react to every little thing. Nina wanted to control those emotions, to keep the pendulum from swinging back and forth, but didn't seem to have the power within herself to do so, though she really did try.

When Nina finally gave her heart to the Lord, she asked Him to take control of her emotional state. He filled her with hope for the first time ever, and gave her the power of the Holy Spirit to overcome her fears. She began to understand the truth—that she didn't have to be ruled by how she felt. With each new bump in the road, she leaned into Him and discovered the joy of abounding in hope, which began to take the place of the emotional roller-coaster ride she'd always known.

Are you on an emotional roller-coaster right now? Lean into Jesus. Trust His work and His Word. He wants you to abound in hope!

Thank You for the reminder that I don't have to be ruled by my emotions, Lord! I can have Your abounding hope! Amen.—JT

MATURE THINKING

Let those of us who are mature think this way, and if in anything
you think otherwise, God will reveal that also to you.
PHILIPPIANS 3:15 ESV

Would you say that your thinking has changed since you were a kid? Back then you were interested in the things that preoccupy all kids—friendships, school, and getting along with your siblings and parents. You probably fretted over things like popularity, grades, and whether or not the boys thought you were pretty. Maybe you were worried about your freckles or your frizzy hair or the goofy clothes your mother made you wear.

The point is, you thought like a child. And now, as an adult, your thinking is completely different. At least, it should be. Once you experience the forgiveness of Christ, you begin to have the mind of Christ, the maturity of Christ. Your focus shifts from self to others. Your goals and plans adapt. Instead of fretting over the things you cannot change, you give yourself over to changing the things you can and accepting those you cannot.

Are you making decisions with more maturity? If not, then take some time to reanalyze your thought-life today. God longs for you to take full advantage of having the mind of Christ.

Lord, I needed the reminder that I have the mind
of Christ. That changes everything! Teach me how
to take full advantage of it, I pray. Amen.—JT

FORGIVEN TO SEE
THROUGH JESUS' EYES

After this, Jesus went out and saw a tax collector by the name of Levi sitting at his tax booth. "Follow me," Jesus said to him, and Levi got up, left everything and followed him. Then Levi held a great banquet for Jesus at his house, and a large crowd of tax collectors and others were eating with them. But the Pharisees and the teachers of the law who belonged to their sect complained to his disciples, "Why do you eat and drink with tax collectors and sinners?"
LUKE 5:27–30 NIV

When Jesus called Levi, the tax collector, to follow Him, it raised quite a stir! The Pharisees and teachers of the law weren't happy that this so-called Savior was eating and drinking with tax collectors and sinners. But Jesus knew something they did not–God loves everyone, not just those living religious, pious lives.

Think about the most sinful person you know, the one who makes your skin crawl. Now see him (or her) through Jesus' eyes. That person is as loved as you are! And Jesus died for that person's forgiveness too.

It's time to see the world through Jesus' eyes of forgiveness and grace. Who can you reach out to today?

Lord, thank You for the reminder that all are in need of the Gospel message, even those I perceive to be the "worst" sinners. Help me share Your love with them, I pray. Amen.–JT

LET GRACE BE GRACE

And if by grace, then it cannot be based on works;
if it were, grace would no longer be grace.
ROMANS 11:6 NIV

Rachelle had a hard time accepting God's grace. She was raised in a home where grace was rarely talked about but good works were touted. As a result, she learned how to perform up to par–or at least give that appearance. In fact, she became so good at performing that she grew rather proud of herself.

It took some time to realize that her own good works couldn't save her. Rachelle finally approached God with humility in her heart and asked for His grace, His forgiveness, His salvation. In that moment, everything changed. Gone was the need to perform. Gone was the desire to prove anything.

Maybe you're like Rachelle. You've lived your whole life trying to behave, attempting to do the right things. You hoped to win the favor of God and man with your good works. It's time to let go of that mentality and accept the grace of your Savior, Jesus Christ. When you do, He'll give you the desire to continue with those good works, but only with the understanding that you can't possibly save yourself, no matter how hard you try.

I'm done trying to save myself, Lord! It's Your
grace that saves me so that I can do great works
for You, not the other way around. Amen.–JT

THAT ALL SHOULD COME

The Lord isn't really being slow about his promise, as some people think. No, he is being patient for your sake. He does not want anyone to be destroyed, but wants everyone to repent.
2 PETER 3:9 NLT

How many people are there in the world, do you suppose? Billions, right? And of those billions, how many are loved by God? How many does He hope will spend eternity with Him? All of them, of course!

The love of God surpasses anything we could begin to comprehend. Think about how much you adore your children or grandchildren, your nieces and nephews. All of the little ones in your life are precious to you, no doubt. Now imagine the heart of God, loving billions and billions of people, all equally. He's the greatest Papa ever!

The Lord longs for the billions to turn to Him so that He can offer them eternal life through the forgiveness of His Son. You can play a role in telling them. You might not be able to touch billions, but there are dozens in your world who need to know, and you're the perfect person to reach them.

Father, I see! I can play a role in leading others to You. If each one reaches one, then billions will come to know! Help me, I pray. Amen.–JT

ALL THE MORE

Now the law came in to increase the trespass,
but where sin increased, grace abounded all the more.
ROMANS 5:20 ESV

What would happen if we lived in a lawless society? Picture all speed limit signs removed, all laws gone. Why pay for groceries when you could steal them? Why stand in line at the store when you could push your way to the front? Why pay a mortgage on your own home when you could take possession of someone else's at no cost whatsoever?

The truth is, laws are put into place for a reason. They are there to protect us. Laws offer a safeguard. But when we behave lawlessly (and let's face it, we all mess up from time to time), Jesus is there to cover our sins. Where our sin increased, His grace abounded all the more.

Nothing you've done is beyond God's forgiveness. Even if your behavior up to this point has been completely lawless, it hasn't crossed an invisible line in the sand. Jesus came to offer new life for all, no matter how dark your trespasses. Accept His grace today and find complete freedom and new life!

Thank You, Jesus, that my sins weren't too big for
Your grace. Where my sin increased, Your grace
abounded all the more. How I praise You! Amen.—JT

EVERY GOOD AND PERFECT GIFT

Every good gift and every perfect gift is from above,
and comes down from the Father of lights, with
whom there is no variation or shadow of turning.
JAMES 1:17 NKJV

Remember how you felt as a child awaiting Christmas morning? Those gifts under the tree had your full, undivided attention. You went racing to the tree in your pj's, ready to tear away the wrapping paper and discover the presents underneath. Once you'd opened each one, you played with them for hours on end. You couldn't seem to let them go.

In similar fashion, God's Word is filled with amazing gifts, just for you. He spent a lot of time picking them out with you in mind. The Lord knows your likes and dislikes, your strengths and weaknesses. He's keen on giving gifts that will actually help you grow and develop in your relationship with Him. (No rusty bikes in the garage for you–God's gifts stand the test of time!)

What gifts are you most grateful for today? His salvation? Joy? The gift of forgiveness? Peace? Love? The gift of a relationship with the Creator of the universe? Take some time to thank Him for choosing to give you the most precious gift of all–His Son, Jesus.

Lord, I'm so grateful for Your many gifts. You've handpicked
them for me, Your forgiven child! How blessed I am.–JT

WILL HE NOT DO IT?

God is not human, that he should lie, not a human being,
that he should change his mind. Does he speak and
then not act? Does he promise and not fulfill?
NUMBERS 23:19 NIV

It's a terrible feeling to get your hopes up, only to have them dashed. People let us down and we're disappointed time and time again. Maybe you've even let others down, so you've experienced the situation from both sides.

Isn't it wonderful to realize that God will never let you down? If He says He's going to do something, He will follow through. That means you can depend on Him, even when you can't put your trust in anyone else. You can let go of the fear that He's going to betray you or hurt you in some way.

God is not like that. Sure, some of your friends have proven to be like that. They've let you down. And yes, some romantic partners are like that. They betray you, break your heart. Sometimes even family members are like that. But not God. He's not a human being, that He should lie. He's your Creator, the Author of your faith, your best Friend. . .and your ever-faithful Companion, the One who forgave you of your sins and offered new life. And He will never leave or forsake you.

Lord, I'm so grateful I can trust You! You've never
lied to me and You won't start now. If You said it,
I know I can believe it. Amen.–JT

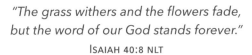

HE STANDS FOREVER

"The grass withers and the flowers fade,
but the word of our God stands forever."
Isaiah 40:8 NLT

Picture a statue standing in a city park. It has been there for years and will be there for decades—perhaps even hundreds of years—to come. Generations come and go, but the statue stands firm, unwavering, even when storms blow through. It's not going anywhere.

In many ways, the Word of God is like that statue. It stands the test of time. It's unchangeable, and it's not going anywhere. In fact, it's even more durable than anything man-made. Generations will pass. Buildings will rise and fall. Flowers will spring to life and then die. Everything will change, morph, twist, and turn. But God will be right there, standing firm amidst it all. He's as solid as a rock, and stronger than the test of time.

If you're struggling with understanding (or accepting) God's forgiveness today, be reminded that the promise of new life isn't a flash-in-the-pan thing. That promise, like all of the promises in the Word of God, stands forever. The Lord won't change His mind about you, you know. You're His. . .forever.

Lord, I'm so glad Your promises stand forever! Years pass.
Generations come and go. But Your Word never changes.
Your promises stand forever. How grateful I am! Amen.–JT

STEADFAST LOVE

The steadfast love of the LORD never ceases;
his mercies never come to an end.
Lamentations 3:22 esv

To be steadfast means you're unwavering. You're like a rock firmly planted in a riverbed. Water rushes over you. . .but you're not moving. You refuse to give up. You dig in and hold on for dear life, no matter how tumultuous things get.

That's what the love of God is like. It's steadfast. When He latched onto you, He did so with the intention to hold on forever. He's like that rock in the riverbed. He's not planning to go anywhere, no matter how far you wander or how tumultuous your emotions get.

What about you? Have the love and forgiveness of God created a steadfastness in your heart? Are you hanging on to Him—and His Word—with all of your heart, mind, and strength? When you live with that sort of determination, others will take note. They will desire the stability of a relationship like that too. They will see the love of God shining in your eyes and the steadfastness deep inside your heart. So hold tight, sister! Don't let the rivers of life uproot you. Don't let go.

I'm so grateful for Your steadfast love, Lord!
Where would I be without it? I'm so glad
I'll never have to find out. Amen.—JT

CRUCIFIED WITH CHRIST

*I have been crucified with Christ; it is no longer I
who live, but Christ lives in me; and the life which
I now live in the flesh I live by faith in the Son of God,
who loved me and gave Himself for me.*

GALATIANS 2:20 NKJV

What does it mean to be crucified with Christ? Have you ever asked yourself that question? It's not like you walked the road to Golgotha, carrying His cross on your shoulders. You didn't hang on the tree or feel the pain of the nails piercing your hands and feet. Your body wasn't carried into the tomb. You didn't rise on the third day. So what does this verse imply?

Being crucified with Christ isn't a physical act. It happens when you accept His work on the cross and apply it to your own life. When you give your heart to Him and receive forgiveness, you are born again. That means your life—your spiritual life, anyway—begins again. You get a second chance, an opportunity to start fresh.

You've been crucified with Christ! He's now alive inside of You. He gave everything so that you could experience this wonderful new journey, from here all the way to heaven. What an amazing Savior!

*Thank You for dying so that I could have life, Jesus. You paid
it all so that I could have it all. How I praise You! Amen.—JT*

COMPLETELY COVERED

*"Blessed are those whose transgressions are forgiven,
whose sins are covered. Blessed is the one whose
sin the Lord will never count against them."*
ROMANS 4:7-8 NIV

According to the *Oxford English Dictionary*, a transgression is "an act that goes against a law, rule, or code of conduct; an offence."

How many transgressions have you committed in your life, do you suppose? A hundred? Two hundred? Thousands? No doubt you've already committed countless acts that created offense over the course of your lifetime, and it's highly likely you'll commit even more before your days on earth are through.

Now picture the blood of Jesus flowing down from the cross. It covers every transgression—not just the ones you committed today, but all of those naughty things you did as a kid. Those selfish things you did as a teen. Those destructive things you did as a young adult. That snarky thing you said to your coworker. That little white lie you told to get you out of a pickle with your boss. The sins you have yet to commit. Jesus' blood covers it all.

The forgiveness of Jesus doesn't give us license to continue sinning, but it truly does cover everything—from the start of your life to the very end. Doesn't it feel good to realize God's got you covered?

*Lord, I'm so grateful my sins are completely
covered. You've forgiven it all! Amen.—JT*

WHILE WE WERE YET SINNERS

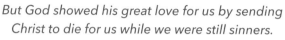

*But God showed his great love for us by sending
Christ to die for us while we were still sinners.*
ROMANS 5:8 NLT

Anne-Marie ran from God from the time she was a teen. As a result, she had a rocky relationship with her mother, a devout Christian. They rarely spoke, even as her mother reached her golden years. There was so much water under the bridge, and all of it tumultuous. Anne-Marie sometimes wondered if engaging her mom in a conversation would solve anything anyway. Mom would just try to convert her, as always.

When her mother passed away, Anne-Marie realized she couldn't get those years back. Regrets shrouded her memories. She was riddled with guilt.

When she entered her fifties, Anne-Marie finally gave her heart to the Lord. How happy her mother would have been, if only she had known. It took some time for Anne-Marie to forgive herself for not making her mother's life easier all those years, but she also celebrated the fact that they would have eternity to make up for the lost time. That knowledge brought peace and comfort.

Perhaps you can relate to Anne-Marie. You wish you could undo the past and recreate relationships. What a blessing to know that eternity awaits!

*Lord, I want to make the most of my relationships with the people
You've placed around me. I don't want to have regrets after the
fact. Show me how to love. . .right here, right now. Amen.—JT*

LIFE IN THE SPIRIT

It is the Spirit who gives life; the flesh is no help at all.
The words that I have spoken to you are spirit and life.
JOHN 6:63 ESV

Take a close look at today's scripture verse. What comes to mind when you read the words "the flesh is no help at all"? Seems impossible, right? We're so used to doing things in the flesh, after all. But God moves supernaturally—above and beyond the realm of the flesh. The words that He has spoken over your life are just that. . .life. They're not dependent on anything you can do (and aren't limited by any bad things you might have done).

The Spirit gives life. And the Spirit gives freedom from the pain of the past. You can live in the Spirit, walk by the Spirit, and enjoy the blessings that come from living a Spirit-filled life. It's a package deal when you come to know Christ and accept His gift of salvation. You don't just receive forgiveness and eternal life; you get to enjoy a supernatural relationship with the very One who created you. Now, that's a gift worth celebrating!

Father, You've spoken life over me. It's supernatural!
My flesh didn't bring it about. Only You could accomplish
life in the Spirit, and I'm so grateful! Amen.—JT

A NEW CREATION

*Therefore, if anyone is in Christ, the new creation
has come: The old has gone, the new is here!*
2 CORINTHIANS 5:17 NIV

Picture a butterfly emerging from a chrysalis. How amazing that first glimpse of sunlight must be. How warm, the sunshine on his wings! The little butterfly tests out his wings, spreads them wide, and takes flight. The first few feet are precarious, at best, but before long he's got the hang of it. In fact, he's doing quite well.

Do you think that butterfly would ever be tempted to retreat back into his chrysalis once he's learned to soar? Of course not! Doing so would be the equivalent of a prisoner returning to his cell once freed.

In many ways, you are like that butterfly. God has forgiven you. He has released you from your proverbial chrysalis. You've spread your wings and taken flight. To turn back now would be counterproductive (and, frankly, depressing). The Lord wants you to move forward...onward and upward. That chrysalis has crumbled to pieces, no longer usable to you. Cast it aside and move on, girl!

*Thank You, Lord, for giving me wings to fly. My chrysalis
days are over! I'm forgiven and free to soar. Amen.–JT*

HAVING DONE ALL. . .STAND

*Therefore take up the whole armor of God,
that you may be able to withstand in the evil
day, and having done all, to stand firm.*
EPHESIANS 6:13 ESV

There really are times in life when you've done everything you can do. You've prayed. You've made the necessary adjustments. You've followed the leading of the Holy Spirit. But things just don't seem to be going your way.

Here's a precious truth from the Word of God—you can still stand even when everything around you is crumbling. In His strength you can keep putting one foot in front of the other, even when you don't feel like it, even when it makes more sense to give up.

Having done all. . .stand. When others tell you to quit. When your dreams don't seem to be coming true. When your heart just isn't in it. When you can't seem to remember that you're truly forgiven.

God didn't bring you this far to leave you now. He saved you, filled you with His Spirit, and called you to great things. He has shown you new life, new hopes, new possibilities. So don't listen if the enemy whispers those dreadful words, "It's over." It's not over. In fact, it's only the beginning.

*Lord, thank You! You've forgiven me and released me
from a life of pain. You don't want me to give up now.
With Your help, I'll keep standing! Amen.—JT*

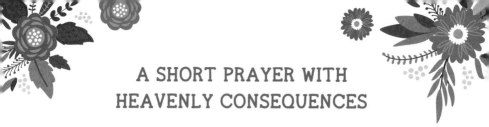

A SHORT PRAYER WITH HEAVENLY CONSEQUENCES

"In the same way, I tell you, there is rejoicing
in the presence of the angels of God
over one sinner who repents."
LUKE 15:10 NIV

If you have never experienced the miracle of grace that only God can give in Christ, we hope you will accept His most magnificent present, which is available to all humankind. You may receive this gift of salvation by asking Christ to forgive you of your sins and then trusting Him as your Savior and Lord of your life. Joy and peace are now yours, as well as eternal life! What a glorious new beginning!

Oh, and feel free to celebrate in a big way. After all, the angels are rejoicing over you!

Heavenly Father, I know I'm a sinner. Thank You for sending
Your beloved Son to die on the cross and save me from my sins.
Please come into my life and lead me today and for all my days
to come. Thank You for the gift of eternal life! Amen.

SCRIPTURE INDEX

OLD TESTAMENT